COLOURFUL BOARDROOMS

Transforming leaders inside and out

Kath Roberts and Kate Griffiths

KK Publishing
Iceni Court, Evolution House,
Delft Way,
Norwich NR6 6BB

http://artofleadership.co

ISBN-13: 978-0-9956929-0-9

ISBN-10: 0995692904

All photography provided by Sharon Cooper
www.sharoncooper.co.uk

Dear Rory

When it feels like the world's gone mad, dip into this for a different perspective — a reminder of the most beautiful world our hearts know is possible.

Love + Magic
Kate

Feb 2019.

Seeking Wisdom

There's a parable that Socrates had a student who asked him, "How can I get wisdom?" Socrates walked him down to the ocean until they were both standing waist-high in the water. Then he grabbed the student's head and pushed it underwater, holding it there while the student struggled and panicked. When he let go and the student stood up, gasping for air, Socrates said, "When you want wisdom as much as you wanted that next breath, you'll get it."

Contents

Foreword

A New Approach

I am fortunate to be one of the many entrepreneurs today running a micro business which allows me to spend my time running a portfolio of exciting projects. At any given time, I might be writing the next book or article, operating as a change consultant in a large corporation, coaching an executive to help prevent them from burn out or working with mid-life women to find their voice.

I chose to move out of what I call the 'Grey Zone' into an environment where I decide how and with whom I spend my time. It takes courage to do something different which is why many people stay in the 'Grey Zone' often for their whole lives. I have been struck by what I call the 'Corporate Zombies' who make the journey day in and day out to their place of work. The majority of them appear to be in a complete trance as they fight their way through the crowds. I wonder what they are thinking and feeling? How many of them dream of a different life as they queue to get on the tube?

Once at your desk you are greeted by heavy expectations of what must be done today before you have to repeat the process all the way back home. Then again tomorrow and the next day and the next day for the next 40 years it continues.

This is what I really enjoyed about Colourful Boardrooms which provides a refreshing alternative to such a grey model of what could be possible in business. In living and working in a way that enables you to breathe again. How does it do this?

We can sense that the old structures are creaking at the seams. Change is happening all around us inviting us to embrace new ways of working. For this to take shape we first require a new energetic level and way of being with one another. The underlying philosophy of the book is that feelings play a vital role in inspirational leadership; emotions are the most overlooked concept in the majority of companies today. The statement is obvious yet the behaviours and practices all suggest this is far from the day-to-day reality and somehow feelings are less important to getting the work done. Kath and Kate turn the spotlight up on the importance of emotions.

They have turned business models upside down and thinking inside out to show leaders how to be far more intentional and conscious in the way they lead thereby building cultures that can help people to thrive.

I am really excited about the way that they use colour to facilitate enhanced creativity. You just can't think it and are therefore more inclined to choose intuitively. It therefore, gets to the heart of the matter in a powerful way.

As an NLP Master trainer I totally understand the importance of positive emotional states to build coherence. When we feel excited about life we typically have a lot more energy, increased creative capacity, a sense of optimism, enthusiasm for our work as well as the self-belief and empathy for others.

This book illustrates plenty of different leadership examples in the various colour sections to demonstrate how you really can change yourself and your teams to expand your perception, align your behaviours and live more whole-heartedly whilst building predictable results.

This book will challenge how you create the cultures of the future that will enable people to thrive not just survive in 'corporate zombie' mode!

Enjoy!

Lindsey Agness
Master Trainer of NLP
Founder of The Change Corporation:
www.thechangecorporation.com
and Age with Attitude: www.agewithattitude.co.uk

Preface

Why us, why now?

Why is there a need for another leadership development book? Or better still, how does this book differ from other books that focus on organisational development (OD)? We explain.

The combination of our unique individual backgrounds, understanding and capacities offers a comprehensive range of experience and skills. Kath got to the top of her game by being one of the first women MDs for an international recruitment firm and Kate set up the first women's network for the UK arm of a global professional services firm whilst developing their public sector Diversity Practice from a standing start. In both instances, we worked in overtly male industries and left our mark.

In different ways both of us have been plucky, risk-taking mavericks who never settled for the status quo. We individually came to the same conclusion around 2008 that we could make it on our own. Before coming together to start running programmes as one, we had established our own coaching businesses, which we continue to run alongside our joint collaboration. Our collaboration models interdependence rather than dependence or independence, both of which are more the norm in the market.

Over the years we have questioned everything we have ever learnt and challenged anything that did not stack up. We never just accept wholesale others' thinking, and in recognition of that, we have been defined as edge walkers. We have each yearned for a new way of doing business that recognises business as the life force of society rather than as the pariah. We take the best of existing ideas such as systems thinking and blend them with our own unique insights as colour therapists and coaches to create something which is new in the field of leadership.

In NLP terms, our way of working brings together the visual, the auditory, the kinaesthetic and the olfactory elements. This is why we get the results that we do, because we immerse participants in experiential learning which scrambles their minds so that they can move out of consensus reality (which focuses on facts and activities) into dreaming and reflection (imagination and qualities associated with being), which enables greater creativity. In the work place and in the views of the leading OD luminaries, there is a propensity to rely on the conscious mind; dialogue closes down because there is too much focus on both winning the argument at any cost and about being right. Through colour, we take people out of the mental plane so that they can get more in touch with their own and others' emotions, thereby building self-understanding, self-awareness and self-acceptance. All this has a major impact on building emotional, social and relationship intelligence and deeper connection within the work place.

As coaches we feel that there is a need for a fresh perspective in leadership and organisational development. To date, most of the seminal works in the field have been written by men with a focus on the next great model. This only takes organisations so far. It is clear that there is leadership deficit and a plethora of unhealthy cultures where employees work to make do and are stuck in an outdated post-industrial model which is replicated across all of our social systems. We, as consultants, are the advocates of oxytocin as opposed to cortisol. Most organisations are flooded with the latter, which translates into management by fear and leads to stress. Oxytocin provides an environment where everyone feels safe so they move away from resistance and see themselves as co-creators of their reality. This means that whilst we emphasise the importance of the global "we", we know that it is realised through recognition of the individual and their uniqueness within "the we". Colour transforms businesses by helping individual leaders understand themselves better so that they can question their motives and behaviours and by providing the meaning behind the story. They can incorporate in their management style, for example, the value of spending the time it takes to get to know their teams because they know that building relationships is the key to developing strong cultures based on an awareness of the collective consciousness. Conscious leadership means being more intentional. This book introduces the background and philosophy of our approach in which we weave coaching and therapy to bring transformation and integration using colour as the principal modality.

CHAPTER 1:

A Short History of our World Post 2008

The old story of separation that is fuelled by a belief in competition and acquisition is breaking down. And a new story is emerging. It's a challenging time in our development as a species. We, as authors, would go as far as to say that the day-to-day decisions that we each make over the next 20 years will determine whether collectively we drive the human race to extinction or find a way through. In response to this challenge, we have developed an approach to increase the levels of conscious awareness in business. Our focus is there, because we see business as the life force of society. Beginning in the next chapter, we will present our toolkit; in this opening chapter, we will explore the factors that have brought us as corporations and humans to this tipping point.

In 2008, there was a major global financial crisis that was a key turning point. Many more people started to question the validity of the old economic paradigm. The crisis, then, is our starting point for understanding how we have come to be in a time of transition. It led to the embryonic forms of change that are emerging now.

As Charles Eisenstein[1] indicated in *The More Beautiful World Our Hearts Know is Possible,* we cannot enter the new paradigm[2] or story without first integrating the lessons from the old paradigm. The rest of this chapter is organised around key themes that show the patterns which have led from the old to the new. The key to entering the new story is to disrupt our sense of busyness, a common trait in business today, and enter into a period of non-doing so we can reflect. Busyness is merely a form of distraction: repetitive actions and habits stop us from seeing what is really important.

From a place of reflection, we can start to appreciate who we really are and regain the ability to act from freedom rather than habit. From that place it is possible to start challenging unquestioned answers that have underpinned Western society for so long.

The happier and more engaged in our work we are, the greater our impact will be, in terms of our ability to affect others positively. When we're doing the kind of work we love, we stop searching and we start being. We've stopped looking outside of ourselves for that fulfilment and happiness and we've become that change in action.

That is why for business transformation to work we must first commence with personal individual transformation. As we begin to change the lens through which we see our world, we start to access higher levels of consciousness that take us straight into breakthrough thinking and being.

How did we get into transition?

To understand the 2008 financial crisis, we need to go back in time. In 1989, Francis Fukuyama published an essay called *The End of History?* His theory was that the great ideological battles between East and West were over, and that Western liberal democracy had triumphed. In 1992 he published his book in which he highlighted:

The end of history will be a very sad time. The struggle for recognition, the willingness to risk one's life for a purely abstract goal, the worldwide ideological struggle that called forth daring, courage, imagination, and idealism, will be replaced by economic calculation, the endless solving of technical problems, environmental concerns, and the satisfaction of sophisticated consumer demands.

Fukuyama did not see all societies becoming Western liberal democracies: his focus was on ideas, not events. He was extending Hegel's argument by changing the end-point from Communism to a universal acceptance that Western liberal democracy could not be bettered. Evidence that supports his viewpoint includes the conversations of activists today, which tend to focus on the levels of CO_2 emissions; and the hordes camped out on the streets of Rio waiting for the first Apple store to open.

At that time, and for a number of years, politics operated in a vacuum (it was the age of the technocrat), but the 2008 financial crisis shook that up to a degree. It was a turning point because it threw into question the unwritten beliefs that had been the fabric of society, in particular the mantra that constant growth is good for business.

Finances: Old Story

The film *Inside Job,* which won the Academy Award for best documentary in 2010, was a synthesis of a number of interviews with many of the key players in the US at the time. It explains why, since 2008, so little has been done to reform the financial world or bring criminal prosecution against the main protagonists by showing the cronyism that existed between academics, politicians and economists that has continued even under Obama's presidency.

The greed of a few created ripples that manifested far and wide, affecting the many. The last decade signified a breakdown of an already creaking system and now more than ever, it is time to dream a new one into being.

Finances: Transitioning towards the New

There is general agreement that the current financial institutions are rigged in such a way as to favour a small percentage of society. There has been a move towards a new way of generating capital for projects. This can be seen through the rise of crowdsourcing as a mechanism for generating the funds to get a book published, to get a film made or a building bought to put to community use.

Our current point in history and the 2008 financial meltdown are direct consequences of our global economic interconnection and interdependence. Pierre Teilhard De Chardin[3] expresses this very well:

The farther and more deeply we penetrate into matter, by means of increasingly powerful methods, the more we are confounded by the interdependence of its parts. All around us, as far as the eye can see, the universe holds together, and only one way of considering it is really possible, that is, to take it as a whole, in one piece.

How do we do this?

We do it by disrupting the existing paradigm, the current story of the world, whilst at the same time telling a new story of the world, so that those in the spaces between the stories have somewhere to go.

Charles Eisenstein suggests that people do not form their beliefs based on evidence or reason initially.

Rather, we use reason to arrange the evidence into a story aligned with an underlying state of being that includes emotional tendencies, old wounds, patterns of relationships and outlook on life. [This interweaves] *with the deep, invisible personal mythologies that define our lives. These personal mythologies in turn are woven into our cultural mythology, the consensus reality that goes as deep as civilization itself.*[4]

In other words, we make up our reality based on our past experiences, some of which are conscious, and many of which are unconscious. To make a shift to create the new story requires us to draw upon our imaginations and to tune into our desires by connecting more consciously to our feelings. We are far closer to this than you may realise.

Modern science reveals to us that through each emotion we experience in our bodies, we also undergo chemical changes in, for example, PH balance and hormones that will mirror those feelings.

And emotion is energy in motion. We need to see the world as pure energy where love is the greatest connector, and fear and hate its greatest detractors. When we bring doubt or judgement into our world, we stop the flow of our own creativity unfolding. The stronger our belief in love is, the easier life becomes, because we tap into the web of energy that is all around us and connects all of us.

Our universe reflects back to us what we have created. When we doubt and judge, we reinforce a sense of separation, and it is at that point that we lose our ultimate connection and harmony to all that exists. We become totally disconnected from nature.

We are now at a tipping point and yet, in many ways, what we are currently experiencing is merely a continuing process of centuries of change and evolution. Some regard our present-day circumstances and obstacles as far less turbulent than those of our ancestors. Many social commentators today point to glaring inequalities across nations, classes and sexes, reinforcing a popular meme that the more things change the more they actually stay the same.

Transformation or change is a given – we are all constantly evolving along with our environments. The cells in our bodies are constantly dying and being created. Our energy fields expand and contract according to our emotional state. We now know that we each have the capacity to build new neural pathways and networks in our brains, irrespective of our age. It is never too late to learn new tricks!

Opportunities have appeared since time immemorial where individuals have sensed and responded to the growing demands for change. And during our time period, for example, a number of millionaires were created in the post-1929 crash because they could take advantage of the lower prices and the fact that bankrupt businesses were being sold for a song.[5] Perhaps this was a result of the growing sentiment and mood of a people whose realisation was that the best way to predict their futures and secure their freedom was to create it themselves.

In nature, we are given perfect examples of radical change and we witness endings and new beginnings all the time as the cycle of life continues. When nature reaches a limitation, it does not necessarily adapt and stabilise; instead it innovates and transforms. Struggles and crises represent the hallmarks of change.

As we move from our current paradigm to a new one, there will be many shifts bringing with them winners and losers. The winners will be those who consciously choose to design and create how they want to be with each other and how they will live and work together. What is crystal clear is the need for us all to learn to live in harmony with our environment.

Now we need to move away from the overly mechanistic, rationalistic and determinist way of doing business, which dominated the last century. We are being offered the chance to reconnect once more with our intuitive intelligence, to our soul's calling, so we can begin to make the holistic connections and quantum leaps to avoid repeating the same patterns of behaviour of the past.

Improved living standards and media output have created increased expectations along with the values of acquisitiveness, materialism and a belief that we must compete to get on in a world where resources are scarce. Yet competition only ever leads to one outcome: winners and losers. We are still, in many regards, finding our feet in how to truly collaborate with others, because collaboration requires far more of us than we ever imagined. Successful collaboration must be done from the heart as well as the head.

Many people are now turning their backs on excessive consumerism and the traditional career paths. They are choosing a different way – an improved quality of life full of meaning and fulfilment, a chance to slow down and achieve more, a chance to acquire less but have far more.

From a financial perspective, downsizing is on the increase with many people reporting increased happiness as a result of reduced hours of working, career changes or stopping work altogether.

Organisations: The Old Story

Morale, motivation, engagement and retention remain priorities for managers and leaders who are short of talent and exposed to an increasingly knowledge-centric environment. The shortage of emotionally and spiritually intelligent leaders only serves to compound this problem.

Whilst a few enlightened employers are able to make the leap to recognising that people make the real difference and thus are thinking differently and more creatively on how to address employee needs, the majority still treat people as a dispensable asset on the balance sheet, eroding further any real loyalty to a brand and inciting the more entrepreneurially inclined to walk free.

With all this in mind, it is time to move our focus beyond work-life balance to work-life integration. When we are able to carry out the work we love to do, invariably we make better partners, parents and colleagues. This kind of purposeful work, imbued with the greatest autonomy and the fullest capacity to master and hone our talents and give our gifts, builds more positive and coherent minds, healthier bodies and altogether happier spirits. This translates directly into a more connected and compassionate society that builds interdependent communities.

Impact of Technology

Another facet that is changing the landscape of organisations today is technology. Whilst technological developments and modern science have facilitated significant life enhancement for many of us, technology itself has made some things more complex and other things easier.

Rapid advancements in technology have created dynamic, yet chaotic, change. The fully connected information age has had a significant impact on the accessibility and breadth of knowledge available to society. This started with the advent of personal computers in the late 1970s and led to the Internet reaching critical mass during the 1990s, creating a necessary global network. In 2015, 2.7 billion people, or 40% of the world's population, were connected to the Internet. Every day, up to 294 billion emails was sent and at least 60 hours of video were uploaded to YouTube every minute.[6] Human knowledge is doubling every ten years and computer knowledge every 18 months.[7] Entire industries and lifestyles are being overturned, giving rise to totally new ones. The work of Technology has released jobs and costs from the corporate sector and continues to do so; increasing job insecurity and uncertainty as more routine tasks are replaced every month by computers and other automated options. Elance, an online employment site, has currently 1.3 million independent contractors registered on their books.

Thomas Frey, a futurist, predicts that two billion jobs will disappear by 2030; this represents 50% of all jobs on the planet. He states that rather than worrying about unemployment, tomorrow's workers will focus on the development of a variety of skills that could keep them working productively and continuously whether there are jobs or not. This feels like a world away from a society where our ancestors were largely dependent upon their employers who owned the tools of production.

The subtle change in relationship between employee and employer is already here, and to many this is proving to be a liberating experience. The pioneers and explorers of this brave new world, with their flow of ideas and technological expertise, have already secured their entry into the rising economic elite, whilst to those whose skills have become obsolete; this is both a distressing and painful time.

We have all witnessed first-hand the information overload that the knowledge age has brought to us as a result of all these new technologies. But it is precisely this information and technology that are creating opportunities everywhere for individuals who want to capitalise on it. Millions of us are beginning to work and live more creatively like artists and scientists always have. Our values, our tastes, our personal relationships, our choices of where we live and even our sense and use of time are changing.

Technological Overwhelm

According to recent research, one third of us feel overwhelmed by technology these days. Our relationship to technology also has a direct impact on the way in which we experience our life as a whole. Neuroscientists confirm that we aren't set up to multitask and it actually tires the brain.[8] When we try to undertake one task at the same time as another, we must switch attention and this directly impacts our concentration levels and performance. Multitasking overstimulates and fatigues the frontal lobe – the part of our brains which regulates problem-solving and decision-making.

Unsurprisingly, this slows down our efficiency and ultimately takes its toll on our overall performance and productivity: a constant concern and preoccupation for all companies. Multitasking also leads to the build-up of cortisol, the predominant stress hormone. Stress leaves us open to all kinds of infections and illnesses as it plays havoc with our immune system.

Perhaps more alarmingly, there are studies that suggest that our interaction with technology has the potential to rewire the way in which our brain operates. Recent research has shown that the sound of a text message arriving or an email hitting your inbox leads to the release of dopamine, a chemical activated when something enjoyable happens unexpectedly. If this is the case, then we could say that overusing technology trains the brain to relate these feelings of pleasure with this kind of interaction, further amplifying our desire to engage with it. The presence and growth of technology

12

has brought with it a whole host of wonderful things and the following additional negative consequences.

A 2001 Stanford University study examining the Internet's effect on socialisation found that for every hour we spend on computers, we cut traditional face-to-face time by nearly half an hour. American neuroscientist Dr Gary Small states that this weakens the brain's neural circuitry, which controls human contact, causing us to misinterpret or miss subtle non-verbal messages. We are losing the ability to truly listen to and really hear people because we are constantly distracted through our multitasking.

Online communication was supposed to create more time and space for creative thinking and facilitate improved wellbeing; in reality it seems to be doing the opposite. The desire to be available 24/7 leads to additional stress and pressure on individuals and an inability to engage fully in anything. In the workplace, this leads to reduced productivity. To quote Sir Cary Cooper, Professor of Organisational Psychology and Health at Lancaster University and previous advisor to the Government Office for Science about mental health in the workplace, *The UK has the second lowest rate of productivity out of the leading G7 industrial nations, putting it behind the US, Germany, France, Italy and Canada but ahead of Japan.* He suggests that the over-reliance on email as a form of communication has been a factor in this phenomenon but he goes on to say that *The UK's development of a macho culture in which employees wanted to be seen to be available by email at all hours is causing stress, depression and having a direct impact on workers' efficiency.*

The *Independent* reports that "Facebook depression" is caused because people tend to publicise only good moments, good photos, and good events in their lives, while hiding the negative ones; users are left with a skewed view of their friends' lives, feeling sad or dull by comparison. Rates of cyberstalking and cyberbullying have significantly increased with calls for social networking sites to do far more about it.

Growing Commoditisation

The growing trend of product and service commoditisation – when something moves from being highly differentiated in its market to being just one alternative among a number of look-alikes the consumer could choose – is forcing the ever-greater need for continued pace of innovation development. Same old same old doesn't work anymore. A commodity market is characterised by the multiple effect of declining prices and margins, increased competition and lower barriers to entry of the sort that technological disruption brings. This allows smaller firms to produce the same quality products and/or services and offer the same functionality as larger firms. These smaller, less bureaucratic businesses are often more agile and faster to market than the traditional provider.

Wholescale disruption through globalisation and the downward trend of prices and margins force companies to outsource particular functions to cheaper parts of the world with local available skills. Witness the rise of India's call centre sector, which grew year on year by 20% before the 2008 global financial crisis. It was largely built on a cost-saving agenda rather than a quality-driven approach and this led to dissatisfaction and deplorable customer service experiences for many Western audiences across the Telecom, Banking and IT sectors.

One could argue that companies had little option when one considers the increasing monotony of this type of work with limited room for variety and initiative taking. This is a reflection of the increasing focus towards specialisation. We have here a prime example of the intensification of segmentation and fragmentation of work, ironically set up to improve response times and experiences but delivering quite the reverse. Thus, the drive for efficiency is leading to the end of low-skill jobs. It's not uncommon now to physically enter a company and instead of seeing a receptionist, you are presented with a computer monitor and are asked to log your arrival on screen!

The above are clear examples of the silo mentality, which leads to an ever-increasing loss of connection in the business world. These solutions are often like sticking plasters covering a festering and bleeding wound. They appear to improve matters short term but because they never get to the root of the matter, they end up creating more chaos and challenges with increasing worldwide ramifications.

Despite the picture painted above, it is not all hopeless. There is a way out of this, and it includes our set of diagnostic tools, *The KK Systems*™,[9] which we will present later in the book. We would like to acknowledge that *The KK Systems*™ as an approach is heavily endebted to Colour Mirrors and Melissie Jolie as the founder of that system. Our focus is on taking this work into an organisational setting which has meant taking some broad, esoteric principles and translating them into business speak.

Currently, many leaders in organisations are dead from the neck down in that they make decisions based on logic and reason. This just further complicates issues. As we will show, when the head and heart function together in a more evolved way of thinking and being, an entirely different set of outcomes can be obtained.

Organisations: Emergence of the New

<u>The Rise in Self-employment</u>

We now have a record number of small firms in the UK: some 5.2 million recorded in 2014 (an increase of 760,000 since 2010), and they now account for 48% of private sector employment. The Global Entrepreneurship and Development Institute rank the UK the most entrepreneurial country in Europe and fourth in the world, and describe it as rich, fertile soil for entrepreneurial activity. Micro firms dominate the small business sector numbers with 76% representing one employee and 20% employing fewer than ten employees. The increase in start-ups and self-employment is not driven by necessity but by desire.

Those who choose to start a business or enter self-employment are doing so because they want to. They view it as an opportunity, rather than feeling they have no other alternative, and it's never been easier to set up a business. In 2014 an RSA populous survey of business owners found that 84% agreed that being self-employed meant they were more content in their working lives and that only 27% of those who started up in the recessionary period of 2008–2012 did so to escape unemployment.

Self-employed people are referred to as business owners, freelancers, consultants and contractors. These are independent professionals who provide important services to a wide range of businesses in different sectors. For them, self-employment is the model they are actively choosing as the best way of using their skills and earning an income. Self-employment provides flexibility and a varied career; it is not the poor cousin of employment.

Welcome to the Transformation Age!

As we begin to place greater focus upon our own inner needs and wellbeing, we are shifting from economic value, as the core, to one of greater emphasis on the growth of human potential, spiritual practice and deeply enriching life experiences.

Here is the golden age where we might all begin to wake up, fully contribute, co-create, live in peace, grow, express ourselves and live in fine health to a ripe old age. This has been foretold: the wise ones of the past, the storytellers, philosophers and mystics predicted this very moment in history. It is a shift from a knowledge-centric information age to a wisdom-based transformation age.

Michio Kaku,[10] a well-known physicist, says it best when he states that *For most of human history we could only watch the dance of nature; however, now we are transitioning to be able to move from being passive observers of nature to being active choreographers of nature. We are moving away from the age of discovery where modern science uncovered the fundamental laws of matter such as Einstein's theory of space-time and Watson and Crick's discovery of the molecular structure of DNA.[11] The next stage is less about unravelling the secrets of nature and more about recognising how powerful we are and so becoming masters of our very own nature.*

The Rise of Cultural Creatives

One third of all US citizens are now reported to create for a living. They can be found across numerous fields and are positively thriving in this new sphere of work. They have been dubbed the "cultural creatives". An additional 80 to 90 million cultural creatives have been identified across Europe since the year 2000. These people are independently-minded, educated free thinkers with a serious focus on spirituality and psychological development as well as fairness and equality with a strong passion for social activism.

This phenomenon has been popularised by books like *The 4-Hour Work Week* by Tim Ferris and Dan Pink's *Free Agent Nation*.

This digital age has given rise to what Marc Prensky has coined the "digital natives" – those individuals born post 1980 into an innate "new culture", while the "digital immigrants" are old-world settlers, who have lived in the analogue age and immigrated to the digital world. Although not complete Luddites, the immigrants struggle more than natives to adapt to hi-tech progress. Connecting with one another in the modern world requires a knack for social networking and texting, which is the norm for the digital native; for the immigrant, however, it can be akin to learning a whole new language.

Complexity Theory

The growing complexity of the challenges we face as a society requires a different way of thinking and being and an entirely different approach to work. Complexity theory offers organisations a way to actually thrive on the ambiguity and unpredictability of modern business. Complexity theory is the study of complex and chaotic systems and how order, pattern and structure can arise from them. Its basic premise is that there is a hidden order to the behaviour and evolution of complex systems.

Organisations are systems composed of people, with a particular emphasis on leaders, who will be at different levels of their own evolution journey – some more than others allowing their egos to lead either consciously or through unconscious projection. But it is exciting to note that when systems become more complex, they can actually take a leap in consciousness and freedom. It takes a small percentage of evolved leaders to impact and influence the other members of the group and at that point, the group is into breakthrough territory. Frédéric Laloux has cited some excellent examples of this type of evolved leadership and consciousness in his book *Reinventing Organizations.*

Work-life Integration

The companies who truly desire a more diverse group of employees are now becoming more appreciative of the fact that a one-size-fits-all policy with regard to typical hygiene factors on pay, benefits, training and development needs will not work in retaining key people. That said, treating people differently is counter-intuitive to a philosophy that suggests treating everyone the same; treating people differently also requires far more consideration and effort in its design, implementation and execution.

As we come to recognise the crucial differentiating aspects for employee retention, we start to move more naturally towards uncovering core intrinsic motivators of employees, which takes us far deeper into both values and vision territories of purposeful work. It is exactly this kind of mastery, depth of purpose, and autonomy that is available to all of us who desire to find more innovative solutions to today's business problems and bring about a more unified and cohesive society for all of us to enjoy.

Community/ Society: Current Paradigm

<u>Demise of Community</u>

Another factor in the story of separation is the demise of community. This can be illustrated using Office for National Statistics data for the UK. When we examine population trends, they paint a clear picture of the disintegration of community. Projecting forward from 2012 to 2032, the populations of 65-84-year-olds and the over-85s are set to increase by 39% and 106% respectively, whereas 0-14 and 15-64 year olds are set to increase by 11% and 7% respectively (source 2001 and 2011 census). Although the impact of an ageing population is hard to predict, The King's Fund extrapolates from data and states that current projections suggest that a high proportion of older people in the future will be living on their own and are therefore likely to require formal care. They go on to say that the number of older people with care needs is expected to rise by more than 60% in the next 20 years.

This puts a massive strain on the NHS, which is already coming apart at the seams. Not surprisingly, one of the few growth industries is the care of the elderly through care homes, specialist retirement villages, and, increasingly, dementia care villages. In many cases, family are still the first port of call for care of the elderly. Recent novels like *Elizabeth Is Missing* highlight the challenges that come when the 40-something husband and wife team both work and have care responsibilities for an elderly parent with some form of dementia. These types of situations are common now because the quality of healthcare in the West is such that we are extending life beyond what was originally possible. All this affects the level of quality time people experience as an extended family unit. It has led to families dumping elderly relatives at hospital for Christmas, claiming they are seriously ill so that they can have break. All these behaviours only serve to expand the level of disconnection between the generations.

Isolation is growing when you look at the changes in the types of households. There is an increase in one-person households from 7.2 million in 2003 to 7.7 million in 2013. An additional 2.4 million people aged between 45–64 live alone, due in part to the increase in the divorce rate and the decline in the number of marriages. The numbers living alone over the age of 65 have increased by 8% to 3.6 million.

Another factor is the number of lone parents, which increased steadily in the ten years from 2001 from 1.7 million to just under 2 million. Lone parents with dependent children represented 26% of all families with dependent children in 2011.

A further pressure on family unity is the ever-increasing cost of living. These rises have exacerbated the requirement for dual income households in order to put bread on the table. Whilst the research is inconclusive, there is strong support for the observation that in families where mothers return to work full-time before their child is one, behavioural issues emerge later on in the child's development and cognitive ability can be affected.

This information helps us understand better the undermining of the social fabric that makes up community. Certainly in the West, nothing has replaced the influence that religion held, and it may be that this has been a significant factor in the uptake of social media usage. This phenomenon has driven separation to even deeper levels; at the very least, it has us questioning what we have come to understand about the definition of a friend.

How did we become such a consumerist society?

There is a very good analysis of this in *The Century of the Self* by Adam Curtis, a BBC series from 2002. It showed very clearly how the work of Sigmund Freud, Anna Freud and Edward Bernays influenced the impact that corporations and governments have had on people and how it ultimately led to the control of the masses. The programme showed how the Freuds and then Bernays were the first to employ psychological techniques to influence the buying behaviours of the mass populous; it showed how Bernays created the need for Public Relations as an industry. The series asked deep questions about the roots and methods of modern consumerism and its implications.

It went on to explore the direct link between the business and the political worlds and how they collaborated to read, create and then fulfil the desires of the public by infusing their products or speeches with mass appeal. Where once the political process was about engaging people's rational, conscious minds, as well as facilitating their needs as a society, the documentary showed how, by employing the tactics of psychoanalysis, politicians appeal to irrational, primitive impulses that have little apparent bearing on issues outside of the narrow self-interest of a consumer population. The essence of the programme is summed up in the following quotation from Paul Mazur, a Wall Street banker working for Lehman Brothers:

We must shift America from a needs to a desires culture. People must be trained to desire, to want new things, even before the old have been entirely consumed.

It clearly documented how we have reached over-consumerism and become both a throw-away society and one riddled with low-level pervasive discontent.

Annie Leonard explores this further in her book, *The Story of Stuff.* She asked herself why there was so much garbage and where it went. This led her to travel around the world following its trail. Her investigations convinced her that the impossible dream of perpetual economic growth and the rampant consumer culture it engenders are the root causes of today's environmental crises.

Climate Change

As we write in 2016, there can be no dispute that the planet is undergoing climate change. And it tends to be presented as a new challenge.

There is a widely held view that global warming is the main reason for the current climate change and that the primary driver is CO_2 emissions. For the first time in recorded history, the global concentration of carbon dioxide in the atmosphere has reached 400 parts per million, according to data from the Mauna Loa Observatory in Hawaii. The prognosis does not look good.

Whilst CO_2 emissions play a part and yes, the closure of the UK's last deep coal pit at Kellingley Colliery in December 2015 goes some way towards reversing the damage caused, this is not the whole story. If we focus merely on climate change and reducing CO_2 emissions, we are perpetuating the story of separation. Think about it for a moment. In 1992 at Rio there was an agreement to stabilise CO_2 emissions to their 1990 levels,[12] and they have increased by 50% – an abysmal failure. We cannot separate out CO_2 emissions from every other facet within the story: everything is connected. Which is more important: the reduction of vehicle-produced CO_2 emissions or deforestation? Look what happened in Pakistan when the Taliban moved into Swat and cut down all the trees. When the rains came, there was nothing to stop the flow and many cities, towns and villages experienced extreme flooding because they had lost their protection.

There is something else happening of which many governments are aware but are refusing to state publicly because they don't want to cause wide-scale panic. That 'something else' is the movement of the North Pole.[13] The website in the footnote plots the current and predicted movement of the North Pole: it appears to be accelerating. Official data on Earth's magnetic field[14] suggests that Earth's magnetic poles are getting ready to flip. Earth's magnetic field was weakening 5% per century, but for more than a decade has been weakening 5% per decade.[15] The current sea level rise has little to do with global sea rise and a lot to do with pole shift[16] as North America moves south towards the bulge of ocean at the Equator. Areas like Florida that are approaching the Equator are sinking,

21

whilst areas moving away from the Equator are rising. Other signs are the rise in the number of erupting volcanoes from three, ten years ago, to around 40 today.[17] In addition, the number of earthquakes has increased from a few 100 ten years ago to 1,492 as of May 2015.[18] There are over 3,500,000 fissures in deep ocean releasing huge quantities of greenhouse gases in far greater quantity than what humans are producing.

Many climate change sceptics blame climate fluctuations on the sun. Most people today would say that the sun is not influenced by human activity. However, if everything is connected and impacts on everything else, is it possible to accept that, just as we are sentient and animals are sentient, that therefore all of nature is sentient? And if so, is it possible to imagine that the Sun is responding to the violence that humanity is perpetuating on Earth? This may sound farfetched, however we now know that trees communicate with each other through scientific experiments conducted by Suzanne Simard over the last 30 years.[19]

Dr Masaru Emoto, an entrepreneur, researcher and author, has produced research that provides some evidence for animism. He discovered that crystals formed in frozen water reveal changes when specific, concentrated thoughts are directed toward them. He found that water from clear springs, and water that has been exposed to loving words, show brilliant, complex, and colourful snowflake patterns. In contrast, polluted water, or water exposed to negative thoughts, forms incomplete, asymmetrical patterns with dull colours. It can therefore be argued that water is alive and has structure and individuality. A mainstream scientist, Gerald Pollack, is now investigating this.

The loud and clear message from climate change is that we are one. What we do to each other, even to the smallest plant or animal, we do to the whole of creation. This is further evidence for Teilhard de Chardin's philosophy about interdependence.

Community/ Society: Emergence of the New

<u>Systems Thinking</u>

The old way of seeing the world is based on the mechanical paradigm that first emerged through the work of Locke and Newton and was the basis for the Enlightenment. Towards the end of the 20th century, this view was challenged by a new approach in the field of business that was presented by Peter Senge. Senge's theories led to the start of a move away from the mechanical paradigm where each part was broken down into its components, and to a call for a more holistic approach in business that has been termed systems thinking. In essence, systems thinking is recognition that each of us is a part of a number of different systems and that with every action we take, we have an impact on the whole.

This connects with the idea of the butterfly effect, popularised by mathematician and meteorologist Edward Lorenz, which is the scientific theory that a single occurrence, no matter how small, can change the course of the universe forever.

Our ideas shape our behaviours and if our ideas about the world in which we operate are mechanical, our behaviours will be different than if our ideas are based on complex adaptive systems, which are more evolutionary and organic. Organisations like society, then, are more like living organisms than machines. From this viewpoint, when looking more deeply at an organisation in its entirety, you begin to see and understand its connecting parts. This more holistic perspective naturally offers a greater chance for cohesion and order. One of the prevailing mantras for systems thinking is "Values plus Vision interspersed with Dialogue leads to Order". This builds on the complexity theory premise that chaos, in the end, always brings order.

By careful observation of the murmuration of starlings in the sky, we witness a high degree of organisation in action which has been called synchrony. For synchrony to exist there are three simple rules[20] which result in perfect harmony and balance: not because there is a specific leader bringing the flock into that state, but because the individual starlings are all interacting and their behaviours are interdependent.

Here is a parable that illustrates the interconnection of all things.

The Little Wave

A little wave is bobbing along in the ocean having a grand old time. He's enjoying the wind and the fresh air until he notices the other waves in front of him, crashing against the shore.

My God, this is terrible, the wave says. *Look what's going to happen to me!*

Then along comes another wave. It sees the first wave, looking grim, and it says to him: *Why do you look so sad?* The first wave says: *You don't understand! We're all going to crash! All of us waves are going to be nothing! Isn't it terrible?*

The second wave says: *No, you don't understand. You're not a wave; you're part of the ocean.*

Source: *Tuesdays with Morrie* by Mitch Albom

Nothing emerges smoothly or consistently. At the same time as the concept of systems thinking appeared in leadership development, there was growing unrest within society. This was captured so well in the emergence of the Occupy Movement. It championed the call for grassroots, creative, non-violent, and direct action to bring needed changes that politicians have since failed to lead on. At its core was a love for the environment, community, humanity, and the planet – a love that trumps temporary financial gain and exposes the shallow aspirations of the destructive aspects of a capitalism which is devoid of compassion, heart, and accountability.

Why wasn't the Occupy Movement sustainable? Why didn't David Cameron's Big Society idea work?

According to Eisenstein, many leftist and environmental groups resemble the groups that they are seeking to replace, in that they have demonstrated the same hunger for power, bullying of underlings and are predicated by ego. In his book, Eisenstein illustrates the point by referring to Orwell's *1984*, where we see that

Winston is no different from the Party – his oppressor – in that he is willing to put the ultimate ends before the means.

Eisenstein goes on to show why the Occupy Movement failed. Realising that some alternatives are no better than what they are replacing, Occupy groups focused on group process in an attempt to implement the egalitarian, inclusive goals they were seeking to bring to society. This led to implosion because the emphasis was on the group and its internal workings, to the detriment of any external goals. What was brilliant about the Occupy Movement was the recognition that the internal and external are linked. It sums up our vision, as authors, which is: who we are and how we relate to each other affect what we create.

Pausing to observe this for a moment as we write, we can see that our society is coming back round full circle to an appreciation of unity consciousness. To give a more substantive understanding of what this means, we have outlined the main elements of M. Scott Peck's four-stage model about the evolution of community as described in his book *The Different Drum.*

1. **Pseudocommunity**: In the first stage, well-intentioned people try to demonstrate their ability to be friendly and sociable, but they do not really delve beneath the surface of each other's ideas or emotions. They use obvious generalities and mutually established stereotypes in speech. Instead of conflict resolution, pseudocommunity involves conflict avoidance, which maintains the appearance or facade of true community. It also serves only to maintain positive emotions, instead of creating a safe space for honesty and love through negative emotions as well. While they are in this phase, members will never really obtain evolution or change, as individuals or as a group.

2. **Chaos**: The first step towards real positivity is, paradoxically, a period of negativity. Once the mutually sustained facade of bonhomie is shed, negative emotions flood through: members start to vent their mutual frustrations, annoyances, and differences. It is a chaotic stage, but Peck describes it as a "beautiful chaos" because it is a sign of healthy growth.

3. **Emptiness**: In order to transcend the stage of Chaos, members are forced to shed that which prevents real communication. Biases and prejudices, the need for power and control, self-superiority, and other similar motives which are only mechanisms of self-validation and/or ego-protection, must yield to empathy, openness to vulnerability, attention, and trust. Hence this stage does not mean people should be "empty" of thoughts, desires, ideas or opinions. Rather, it refers to emptiness of all mental and emotional distortions which reduce one's ability to really share, listen, and build on those thoughts, ideas, etc. It is often the hardest step in the four-level process, as it necessitates the release of patterns which people develop over time in a subconscious attempt to maintain self-worth and positive emotion. This stage should be viewed not merely as a "death" but as a rebirth – of one's true self at the individual level, and at the social level of the genuine and True Community.

4. **True Community**: Having worked through Emptiness, the people in the community enter a place of complete empathy with one another. There is a high level of tacit understanding. People are able to relate to each other's feelings. Discussions, even when heated, never get sour, and motives are not questioned. A deeper and more sustainable level of happiness obtains between the members, which does not have to be forced. Even, and perhaps especially, when conflicts arise, it is understood that they are part of positive change.

What is exciting is that we can now capture glimpses of True Community in the world today whilst acknowledging that many communities are still in Emptiness, Chaos or Pseudocommunity.

Education: Current Paradigm

Education is a microcosm of society. The ever-increasing focus on statistics in education has led to the enaction of the lowest common denominator principle. The dumbing down to ensure that students pass their stats has taken priority over a more person-centred, creative, topic-based approach. It has also meant a tacit acceptance of mediocrity instead of enabling each student to reach his/her potential.

The knock-on impact in business is that the one-size-fits-all model, which the educational system uses, has become the norm, leaving very little room for the development of innovation and creativity within the workplace. Hence the rush of business books in the late 1990s like *The Innovator's Dilemma,* in which Clayton Christensen suggested that successful companies can put too much emphasis on customers' current needs and fail to adopt new technologies or business models that will meet their customers' unstated or future needs. He posits that such companies will eventually fall behind. Christensen calls the anticipation of future needs "disruptive innovation" and gives examples involving the personal computer industry, milkshakes and steel mini-mills.

Education: New Story

Frédéric Laloux gives detailed examples of schools that are working from the principles of the new paradigm in his book, *Reinventing Organizations.* The most extreme and well known are the self organised learning environments (SOLE) where children can work in groups, access the Internet, follow up on a class activity or project and are allowed to see where their interests take them. The term SOLE was popularised by Sugata Mitra. In this setting, the role of teachers changes, as teachers transform into facilitators who facilitate the learning of their students.

Whilst there are some concerns about SOLE, its founding principle that children are intelligent beings that should be given more of a say in their education has permeated many forward thinking establishments today. Sadly, in England, due to the constraints imposed by the national curriculum, most of this creativity is only found in the independent schools sector where there is more latitude to choose what and how subjects are taught. There are now pockets of innovation where everything from literacy to maths and art is treated from the focus point of a specific term theme. As well as taking this more holistic approach to learning, education is also differentiated to accommodate the different ability levels within a group without streaming children into different ability groups.

The New Story/Our Story

The growing trend of individualisation and individuation is a natural outflow of the digital era and globalised world. Individualisation and individuation are not the same things.

<u>Individualism</u>

Individualism, as defined by Wikipedia, is the moral stance, political philosophy, ideology, or social outlook that emphasises the moral worth of the individual. Individualists promote the exercise of their own goals and desires; they value independence and self-reliance, and advocate that interests of the individual should have precedence over the state or a social group; they oppose external interference upon their interests by society or institutions such as the government.

Individualistic behaviour and the growing importance of self and the consequent limited regard for traditional structures is an obvious symptom of our consumer-obsessed reality. One of the consequences of the digital world that we have all come to embrace is the level of personalisation it affords us. From websites that remember our purchasing history to the focused ads that pop up on screen that reflect our browsing habits, our expectations have been raised about what we want and can have.

Personal branding is a consequence of such individualism, self-reliance and self-importance, whereby the need to stand out in the job marketplace as unique and memorable is a necessary aspect to thriving in the ever-changing workplace. If there is nothing unique about our skills, then we quickly become the commodity. Such a change of mindset, where a worker becomes a personal brand, has its appeal because it conveys the idea that we are not just defined by our job and that a company doesn't own us.

The demand for more, fuelled by individual status symbols and aspirational goals driven by constant media campaigns about who we need to be and how we need to look, builds an ever-growing separation of the individual self from its spiritual aspect; this leads to inner conflict giving rise to a whole host of addictions and illnesses termed "lifestyle illnesses." From this place, it is little wonder that wellbeing suffers and that some people are eventually led to reappraising their lifestyle goals.

Growth of the Personal Development Industry

We need only look at the acceleration of the personal development industry to understand this trend. The term "personal development" was coined in the US during the late 60s and early 70s. It emerged as part of California's vogue for self-discovery and life transformation, along with a host of other self-help therapies such as Neuro-Linguistic Programming (NLP), gestalt therapy and family therapy. By the late 1970s and early 1980s, personal development had flourished into a lucrative industry. This pre-empted the emergence of therapy celebrities like Tony Robbins and Jim Rohn, who took centre stage as self-help pioneers of the century, following in the footsteps of giants who had gone before such as Napoleon Hill and Earl Nightingale.

In 1937, Napoleon Hill published the original version of *Think and Grow Rich*. This bestselling book is based on Hill's 25 year study of the 500 wealthiest people in America at the time. Hill was given a journalism assignment to interview highly successful people and write a series of articles on what made those people wealthy and successful. He decided he would call on the world's most powerful and wealthiest man of his time, Andrew Carnegie.[21] And in 1908, by a stroke of luck, he was invited to Carnegie's office to discuss the article. This is where he learnt all about the power of the mind, a basic tenet of which is: what you begin to focus on expands, because energy always follows thought. (Today, quantum physics, metaphysics, NLP and shamanism all teach us the same thing.) Thus Hill's stroke of luck in being invited to speak with Carnegie was in fact synchronicity and the perfect illustration of a mind attuned to a focus. Every day, whether we realise it or not, we make things up and in so doing dream our world into being. The more inspired we are, the more energy we have available to convert an idea from the mental plane of possibility into a plan of action, which translates into the physical plane of reality. For ideas to materialise, they must first be infused with "energetic magic" (positive emotions that inspire, engage and positively move people). We know through history that those leaders who have had the greatest capacity to imagine have generally attracted the greatest following.

As authors, we have already highlighted, that something is stirring in mass consciousness today as more and more people are beginning to wake up. These individuals desire to live and work more consciously and now they have the means and the tools to do so. Many are enthused by the prospect of reaching their full potential and by wanting to understand themselves more deeply and act more authentically as a result. If the last century was characterised by the exploration of outer space, then this promised new golden era must surely be about the exploration of our inner space.

The Next Steps from Our Perspective

<u>Individuation</u>

Individuation is the first step to take to move beyond mere survival for those who are seeking happiness, fulfilment and self-actualisation. The pursuit of self-knowledge and an interest in one's inner space is nothing new: any number of philosophers and teachers of wisdom have told us that the route to our success is an inner game. But what is of paramount significance for the evolution of mass consciousness – of all of us – today is that we are looking at the perfect tipping point conditions towards this possibility. "Individuation" was a term that was first developed by Carl Jung and refers to the psychological process of integrating the opposites, including the conscious with the unconscious parts, and even though integrated, these parts still maintain their relative autonomy. Jung considered individuation to be the central process of human development and therefore a critical step on the path to self-actualisation.

Our business approach uses colour to facilitate introspection by individual leaders' to bring about sustainable organisational development. The initial focus is on uncovering a leader's top individual intrinsic motivators as well as assessing their team's core motivators. This gives a fuller and deeper appreciation of inner drivers and level of energy/appetite for change. We reject the established personality profiling tools because we understand the complexity of human nature and know that leaders are constantly evolving. We therefore try to avoid anything that may stereotype or label individuals as this type or that. The more we have been able to support leaders to work in alignment with their inner motivations, the more we have noticed greater engagement and personal satisfaction in their work.

Self-actualisation is the first step because it is as much about inner peace, meditation and mindful conscious living as it is about obtaining financial freedom and independence. The more we come to understand ourselves and gather the necessary self-acceptance, the greater our capacity and understanding will be for unity and interdependence – a natural development of individuals who have already accessed their own independent spirits and moved away from group conformity. This desire for personal enlightenment has given rise to many branches of psychology and new methodologies to access inner states of heightened consciousness.

Transpersonal Psychology is a school of psychology that integrates the spiritual and transcendent aspects of the human experience within the framework of modern psychology. It could also be defined as a spiritual psychology. The transpersonal is defined as experiences in which the sense of identity or self extends beyond the individual or personal to encompass wider aspects of humankind, life, the psyche or cosmos. Issues considered in Transpersonal Psychology include spiritual self-development, self beyond the ego, peak experiences, mystical experiences, systemic trance, spiritual crises, spiritual evolution, religious conversion and altered states of consciousness, spiritual practices, and other unusually expanded experiences of living. The discipline attempts to describe and integrate spiritual experience within modern psychological theory and to formulate a new theory to encompass such experience.

Ken Wilber's integral theory[22] is a very clear example of this holistic approach to human and societal development. His framework is a key reflection of conscious evolution.

Preoccupation with Wealth Creation

Many wealth creation models encouraging new ways of generating income and accessing time and financial freedom have captured these twin trends of individuation and individualism beautifully. This has happened to a greater extent in the US but the impact is still global. Two good examples are Robert Kiyosaki and Roger

Hamilton. Kiyosaki is a financial advocate, entrepreneur, investor, author and speaker, whose foundation work *Rich Dad Poor Dad* has been simultaneously number one on the top ten bestseller lists in *The Wall Street Journal, USA Today*, and *The New York Times*.

Hamilton, a Hong Kong born, a *New York Times* bestselling author, futurist and social entrepreneur, is considered to be Asia's leading wealth consultant. He was one of the pioneers in early Internet sales communities, having worked for a period of time at Dell Inc. He created a clever profiling system called Wealth Dynamics for Entrepreneurs, which uses a psychometric tool based on the principles of the I Ching. Since its inception, over 250,000 entrepreneurs around the world have used it. As does our approach, it uses colour to highlight different levels of wealth and the characteristics of each. Its colour philosophy is not a thousand miles away from our approach to colour in business, which also pinpoints and demonstrates a leadership consciousness model and which illustrates the levels of thinking and the corresponding behaviours and emotions that lie behind them.

Our colour for business diagnostic tools, henceforth referred to as *The KK Systems™*, have some similarity to Hamilton's talent dynamics in that we firmly believe the individuals who are able to follow a path of least resistance can truly find their flow and operate productively and effectively. We show leaders how to integrate their whole selves and in doing so, achieve quantum leaps and authentic success. We have developed a set of core, foundational colours that work with a set of transitional colours. In Chapter 3, we start to examine the initial core colours.

Co-creation

As we humans begin to appreciate that we are the ultimate co-creators of our reality, we don't need to be at the mercy of past events. We can consciously construct our lives in a way that is in harmony with all aspects of ourselves. If we grasp this aspect of personal transformation, we can start to shape our business environments and relationships in a way that is the fullest expression of who we really are. In our authentically aligned power we can begin to direct our futures in whichever way we choose.

Concluding thoughts

In this opening chapter, we, as authors, have shown that the disintegration of community is a reality – the old mechanisms which bound us together have broken down and been discredited. This can be seen through the rise of polemical works such as *The Selfish Gene* by Richard Dawkins on one end of the spectrum, and a search for meaning found within a growing interest in spirituality on the opposite end. In 1944, Max Planck, the father of quantum theory,[23] shocked the world by saying that the "matrix" is where the birth of stars, the DNA of life, and everything between, originates. Recent discoveries reveal dramatic evidence that Planck's matrix is real. Gregg Braden articulates this very well in *The Divine Matrix.*

We have highlighted throughout this chapter examples of where and how the old story is being disrupted. You can see an example of the new emerging story in the conclusions we draw about climate change. What we do to each other, even to the smallest plant or animal, we do to the whole of creation. We are in the process of a paradigm shift from the old story of separation, to the new story of inter-being. Tools like complexity theory and systems thinking extend this awareness to a wider audience.

We, as authors, have also noted the fact that we appear to have come full circle back to a sense of unity. We have moved from the agrarian age, largely centred around small village communities where any alternative philosophies such as the Cathar movement and Judaism were brutally stamped out by the prevailing authority at the time – the Catholic Church – to scientific determinism under Newton, which brought about a prevailing world view that only things that could be empirically measured and quantified had meaning. Whilst technological and industrial progress continued to be made, this came at the expense of innate individual sentient capabilities. Humanity began to lose its sense of connection to nature and much of the ancient tribal wisdom was vilified. The predominant world view encouraged a separation, which in one sense fitted an industrial age perfectly in that everyone knew their place and role, and greater efficiencies could be realised through the streamlining of processes.[24] This model perpetuated a survival-of-the-fittest mentality where those with the means and the wealth were able to lift themselves above the masses; this has been reinforced by 20th century economic principles.

There now exists a yearning to remember and unlearn so we can yet again tap into the magic and the mysticism of the Universe. As Arthur Koestler wrote, *Magic is simply the science we don't understand yet.* There is a growing acceptance that we live in a sentient universe; Dr Emoto's research into water has helped show this, as has Suzanne Simard's research into trees.

Present-day emphasis on neuroscience is helping us to better understand the brain and its impact on behaviour and cognitive functions. Progressive educationalists and psychologists are leading the way in revealing that there are multiple types of intelligences,[25] which has been further highlighted by the work of Sir Ken Robinson and books such as *The Gift of Dyslexia* by Ronald Davis. It is now well understood that we have more than one brain. Paul MacLean's theory of the triune brain was documented in his book published in 1990 and he was credited with establishing the parameters for investigating the evolution and functioning of the emotional brain. His work also gives greater validity to a growing consciousness and appreciation that we are far more than our minds.

The intuitive mind is a sacred gift and the rational mind is a faithful servant. We have created a society that honours the servant and has forgotten the gift ~ Albert Einstein.

We end this chapter by recalling the ancient Amazon prophecy that speaks of human societies splitting into two paths – that of the Eagle, and that of the Condor. The path of the Condor is the path of heart, of intuition, and of the feminine. The path of the Eagle is the path of the mind, of the industrial, and of the masculine.

The prophecy says that the 1490s would begin a 500-year period during which the Eagle people would become so powerful that they would virtually drive the Condor people out of existence. This can be seen in the conquering of the Americas and the slaughter and oppression of the indigenous peoples in the subsequent 500 years – up to and including today.

The prophecy says that during the next 500-year period, beginning in 1990, the potential would arise for the Eagle and the Condor to come together, to fly in the same sky, and to create a new level of consciousness for humanity.

The prophecy only speaks of the potential. It is up to us to activate this potential and ensure that a new consciousness is allowed to arise. In Chapter 2 we start to reveal what this means.

Notes

1. Charles Eisenstein is a teacher, speaker, and writer focusing on themes of civilization, consciousness, money, and human cultural evolution. He is the author of many books.

2. By 'new paradigm', we mean a new way of thinking that is initially rejected as a concept that is too "out there", and then it becomes accepted by more and more people until it becomes the norm.

3. Pierre Teilhard de Chardin (1881-1955) was born in France and ordained a Jesuit priest in 1911. Trained as a paleontologist, Teilhard de Chardin did research at the Musée National d'Histoire Naturelle in Paris and fieldwork in China, where in 1929 he codiscovered the celebrated "Peking Man" fossils. In his writings, he sought to reconcile his spiritual and scientific beliefs, producing a vision of man as evolving toward the divine. His unorthodox theological positions were at odds with Catholic doctrine and led to a strained relationship with Jesuit leaders, who forbade him from publishing his writings.

4. Charles Einstein (North Atlantic Books, 2013) *The more beautiful World our hearts know is possible*

5. In the following article there is a list of 10 people who made good money post the 1929 crash https://goo.gl/YgHrDF

6. For live stats on the number of internet users and the use of twitter, youtube, emails and more per second go to http://www.internetlivestats.com/

7. David Schilling's article pulls together a number of sources that relate to this phenomenon from Buckminster Fuller to IBM - https://goo.gl/G3cPzG

8. Gloria Mark, professor in the department of informatics at the University of California, Irvine, is quoted in the following article as saying that when people are interrupted, it typically takes 23 minutes and 15 seconds to return to their work, https://goo.gl/hVRpDn

9. *The KK Systems™* so named because we are Kath and Kate but also because the bottles are kinaesthetic keys and they represent our colour framework for business.

10. In *Visions,* physicist and author Michio Kaku examines the great scientific revolutions that have dramatically reshaped the 20th century – the quantum mechanics, biogenetics, and artificial intelligence – and shows how they will change and alter science and the way we live.

11. Friedrich Miescher was the first to isolate DNA in 1869.

12. This is because greenhouse gases -gases that consist largely of CO_2 - are seen to be responsible for global warming.

13. See http://www.ngdc.noaa.gov/geomag/data/poles/NP.xy to see the current and predicted accelerating movement of the position of the North Pole.

14. http://magneticreversal.org collates data from NASA, NOAA, ESA and similarly reputable organisations on the Earth's magnetic field.

15. Further information can be found at http://www.livescience.com/46694-magnetic-field-weakens.html

16. A pole shift is a flip in the Earth's magnetic field where the north and south poles exchange places

17. http://www.volcanodiscovery.com/erupting_volcanoes.html

18. http://earthquake.usgs.gov/earthquakes/map/ - Use the cog in the top right-hand corner, select Magnitude 2.5 and worldwide to see how many earthquakes there have been in the past month.

19. Detailed information can be found at http://www.ted.com/speakers/suzanne_simard.

20. The three simple rules in flocking are:
   1. Separation - avoid crowding neighbours (short-range repulsion)
   2. Alignment - steer towards average heading of neighbours
   3. Cohesion - steer towards average position of neighbours (long-range attraction)

21. Carnegie was the world's first recorded billionaire. He gained his wealth by founding the Carnegie Steel Corporation.

22. Ken Wilber's Integral Theory is an attempt to place a wide diversity of theories and thinkers into one single framework. It is described as a "theory of everything".

23 "All matter originates and exists only by virtue of a force, which brings the particle of an atom to vibration and holds this most minute solar system of the atom together. We must assume behind this force the existence of a conscious and intelligent mind. The matrix is a web of energy that connects everything." This may feel far-fetched to some; however, just to cite one concept, the Hopi Indians' creation story, which is part of ancient wisdom, explores this concept. This is, therefore, not some newfangled notion.

24. Cf. the modern growth of Six Sigma, continued improvement programmes and more recently Agile

25. Howard Gardner (Basic Books, 1983), *Frames of Mind: The Theory of Multiple Intelligences*. Gardner articulated eight criteria for a behaviour to be considered an intelligence: Musical, Visual-spatial, Verbal-linguistic, Logical-mathematical, Bodily-kinaesthetic, Interpersonal, Intrapersonal and Naturalistic. Later he suggested that existential and moral intelligence might also be worthy of inclusion.

CHAPTER 2:

The Psychology of Colour and Its Impact on Modern Day Leadership

Our founding principle regarding leadership is that human beings are informed by the internal AND the external world. Building on the premise that there is no separation, we, as consultants, believe that all transformation starts on the inside and reveals itself on the way out. True business transformation can only take effect when individuals in the organisation have begun to transform their own level of reality.

Today's business world is characterised by whatever is the latest fad or trend that may lead to breakthrough performance. One of the key reasons that 70% of all change projects typically fail is because of the over-emphasis on the exterior world. There is a preoccupation with doing and the implementation of the new without first giving sufficient attention to how people are feeling and why change is necessary. We have chosen Brexit as an example. There was discontent with the way that the EU operated – this had been festering for years coupled with an undercurrent of dissatisfaction with the status quo. Looking at this from a systems perspective, there was tension within the relationship with views ranging from the out-and-out racist perspective of the far right to the liberal educated left, with other outliers who were sick of sucking up the inequality that they perceived and getting little return. These outliers felt that the balance of power had been lost and that there was no outlet for their views. In a system where individuals feel they are not heard or understood, their tendency is to react more strongly in order to bring about change – in essence the protest vote.

Change tends to come in two forms: the evolutionary one or the radical revolutionary one. The latter emerges when society feels deeply repressed and cannot make its voice heard. There have been signs of discontent in our relationship with the EU for decades, but the majority has dismissed it to keep the peace. But at what cost? When a certain part of society is unable to see the gold cage it has created for itself, it leaves no other option but "destructive" change. This has led to fear and it includes a petition to request another referendum, as there is a voice within the system that is struggling to come to terms with what has happened.

Another way of looking at this is to see it as death to the old so that there can be a rebirth or birth of the new. This is a process that has been perpetuated over the centuries. What is needed now is to trust that order will emerge from chaos. Who will benefit from the UK remaining in the EU? Ultimately, in the short term, we have all lost from the UK's decision to leave the EU with the devaluation of the pound and the fluctuating share price. However, if we can ride this storm and the uncertainty that comes with it, understanding that all that is happening is coming out because of the depth of the feelings, then we can start to create a new order that hopefully is better for all.

From an NLP perspective, humans see the world not as it is, but as they are. Our level of perception is made up of personal experiences, our values, our beliefs, and meta-programmes. In other words, the interior world of memory and imagination drives external behaviour and results. Individuals who have woken up to seeing beyond the five-sense experience have a broader reality. Many classify this as magical or mystical. An understanding which we propose as coaches is that this is nothing more than a soul awakening or an individual progressing rapidly to self-actualisation.

Our approach: going beyond models

There are a number of pre-conditions to self-actualisation. One is: it doesn't matter what environment you are in, because it is who you are and how you see the world that matters AND yet, your environment impacts on you and shapes your thinking. The wrong environment can impede your progress and slow down your ability to create your reality. This means it is vital to step away from conformity and the agreed way of thinking on a particular issue in order to get the real breakthroughs. However, this is challenging. Why is that so? Because we are hardwired for negativity instinctively – that is what has enabled us to survive sociobiologically – so whilst we understand the need for change at a logical level, often there is resistance at the feeling level. And it is not just about the feelings on an individual level; it is also the collective feelings and the impact they have in the organisation, and these are contagious. But feelings are so disregarded in business. The recognition of the importance of feelings is a key tenet of the work we, who are both coaches, orchestrate in business.

Stepping back is what helps us see the bigger picture. From an organisational perspective, we'll use the example of Blockbuster, the video chain that became an irrelevance and went to the wall because it did not update its offering in line with the technological changes in society. In other words, whilst we are advocates of focusing on the interior world to build positive states of intention and alignment; we also know that you need to scan and respond to the external environment with appropriate action. It is vital to be aware that our external reality feeds into our internal reality and vice versa.

The second pre-condition of personal transformation and owning our authentic power is, ironically, that we need to show up in our full vulnerability. The more we open up and reveal the full extent of our fragility, the more we can release our own particular scent and hue, thereby attracting a following. As we allow our own uniqueness to flow out, the more the work and accolades flow. In contrast, the more we yearn for the acknowledgement and the accolades, the less we get them.

To fully model vulnerability, you need to be willing: willing to not know but to trust, to let go of the knowledge and how things should be and be completely open to what might be trying to happen in any given moment. And this is a courageous act. It is what separates wise leaders from knowledgeable ones. When you're not afraid to live your life on the edge where you make the rules up as you move along, you experience an altogether different type of freedom, which is exhilarating and intoxicating. Conversely, as you model your vulnerability, your people see your humaneness and you obtain that elusive presence so badly desired by leaders and so needed to inspire organisations.

The philosophy that underpins all of what we, as coaches, do is the belief that deep down, maybe only at an unconscious level, everybody truly knows their purpose and through *The KK Systems*™ and the facilitation that we bring, we help that to emerge by shifting the obstacles (conscious and frequently unconscious negative emotions) that block access to that. We help leaders to access their spiritual intelligence to promote inspiration, unity, collaboration and their connection to the whole. When leaders are living their lives on purpose, there is true alignment within organisations, as they can see and embody certainty within the uncertainty. We help organisations develop empowering cultures by letting go of the need to control everything. We support boards to build congruency between their words and actions and recognise that trust is the glue that holds all this together.

The third pre-condition is that learning that is integrated and that transforms hearts and minds is experiential. Whilst we quote many theorists and models within our work, we have a keen appreciation of that. Working with colour is not about learning by numbers: there is no end to the learning because there are always greater depths or new hues to explore and discover.

As you approach our work, we invite you to try on the learner mindset. You are always at choice whether you take the position of the knower or the learner. You will gain much more if you can remain open even when challenged and you will also gain much more if you get curious about exploring and wondering what a certain trigger is all about rather than closing down and dismissing it.

Here is a question for you. As you reflect on your leadership experiences up to this point: when things were going well for you what did it feel like? How much was the flow that you were in down to the fact that you were enjoying yourself and having fun? We like to think of playfulness as the new mindfulness, and just as babies and young children learn mostly through play, so do we as adults – if we allow ourselves to.

As you read Chapter 1 where we outlined the key trends in our society and the complexity of the challenges that we now face, you may have felt yourself start to go into overwhelm and begun asking yourself, "What's the point?" and/ or "What's my contribution?"

There has never been a greater call for self-leadership[1] than there is today. It is our hope and intention with this book to give you some of the keys that will help you become the leader you were destined to be. We can offer leaders transformation because we pull together many individual strands of leadership development and weave them into a unique, integrated blend that eradicates self-limiting belief constructs. Our approach can be compared to a beautiful tapestry with many intricate strands – a timeless creation which has emerged out of many hours of loving attention. It incorporates embodiment, somatic coaching, NLP, neuroscience, mindfulness, Emotional Freedom Technique (EFT), Gestalt, Transactional Analysis and Transpersonal Psychology. As system workers, our focus is on a holistic way of being and we go further than that, because we are shaping a new paradigm of living and working. Rather than defaulting under the old paradigm of business to playing out the roles of either the victim, the persecutor or the rescuer, we invite in a new paradigm and way of being that encourages leaders to let go of the judgements they hold by taking full responsibility because they now recognise that they create the whole of their realities. We are influenced by many ancient wisdom traditions that have been lost until recently – in particular Shamanism and metaphysics – and we bring them out in our work. Many practitioners find one tool and feel that they have discovered the solution to help businesses transform. What we have realised is that our clients are complex and need a multi-layered approach; we are able to provide a stretch and range that offer a powerful way in, because we have deeply immersed ourselves in the work and integrated our spiritual selves with our emotional, mental and physical selves. Why leaders and organisations sometimes struggle to see the value that colour brings is because they endeavour to access it from the mental or emotional level initially, whereas we are asking them to step up and meet us on a spiritual level first. Colour is the great accelerator which over time brings integration on every level because it allows an individual to understand their whole self, see their uniqueness and heighten their self-awareness to such a degree that they get the best out of every situation. The attributes and properties of each colour cause a shift in energy.

On so many fronts, leadership is considered to be about taking action to make a difference. The decisions you make have an influence on the systems of which you are a part. This may not always be visible to you, but it's there. What if you were to consider something that may appear counter-intuitive – what if you were to consider the opposite? Rather than focusing your energy on doing, notice what happens when you pay attention to who you are becoming. For us, as authors, it is recognising that leadership is as much about what you omit to say as it is about what you actually say. It's about taking time to observe all the underlying patterns within you and your wider organisation and landscape of operation. The pause to reflect to fast forward is sadly underutilised in business today and yet it is a crucial characteristic of any learning organisation.

The moment we can question our reality, we can let go of old belief constructs built on past experience which don't serve the present or future. A recent piece of work we undertook involved supporting a leadership team of a start-up organisation in a reasonably competitive market sector. The underlying assumption of the CEO was that he would have 25% attrition each year because that was the industry standard. As he began to slow down and reflect, he started to pay greater attention to his unconscious assumptions and, in doing so, he was able to completely change his mode of being and way of thinking. What followed was a fundamental rethink and shift which allowed him to recognise that all talent needs to be treated both equally and uniquely, and that this facilitates full retention as opposed to the self-fulfilling process of 25% attrition. Intention moves many possibilities through time and space when it is infused with loving enthusiasm and belief about what's possible. To do this, a willingness to let go of the rule book is required. This is more challenging than it sounds because a number of unquestioned assumptions have existed in the leadership space for years based on a belief in the need to create a "performance culture". For example, organisations like GE and McKinsey have a reputation for culling a percentage of their workforce every year in the name of being effective. They see it as getting rid of underperformers to remain efficient; we see it as a sure way to instil fear and compliance in the workforce.

Our work in many regards is beyond models. People have always seen the need for models in order to make sense of their world, and these models often quickly become obsolete or just don't work: they need to be constantly revised so that individuals and organisations don't get stuck in only one mode of functioning. We offer pay and benefits as just one example of models that have become the norm but that don't really work in an ever-evolving economy. Extrinsic motivation, that is being engaged in an activity to earn a reward,

42

worked in an industrial society that needed security and longevity of employment after the Great Depression and two world wars. It doesn't fit a more sophisticated, knowledge-based environment where individuals know their worth and are intrinsically motivated in other ways.

Vision and values offer us a means to construct a framework of being with one another. New paradigm businesses and those that will thrive in the future, however, will be those that can live in constant re-creation of both self and the collective organisational culture.

We would describe our work, therefore, as less about teaching through knowledge and far more about helping leaders and organisations increase their learning through wisdom. As the saying goes, *Knowledge speaks but wisdom listens*. Knowledge represents the accumulation of facts and data that we have learnt about or experienced. Knowledge is really about the facts and ideas that we acquire through study, research, investigation, observation, or experience. Wisdom on the other hand, is the ability to discern and judge which aspects of that knowledge are true, right, lasting, and applicable to our work and life. It's knowing what to apply and what to leave out. It's also deeper; it's knowing the meaning or reason; and it's about knowing why something is, and what it means to your life. Insight is the deepest level of knowing and the most meaningful to your experience. It means grasping the underlying nature of knowledge, and it is the essence of wisdom. Insight is a truer understanding of your life and the bigger picture of how things intertwine.

What an ever-evolving economy needs is relationship intelligence where the focus is on compassion, connectivity and curiosity. This comes when you tap into the right brain and it is facilitated through the use of creativity and metaphor. We find that parables are excellent ways to explain concepts that may well be new to you, our reader. We will be giving examples of parables regularly: here is the second. The following parable is an introduction to states of consciousness and the role of colour within them.

Colours of the Rainbow

Once upon a time the colours of the world started to quarrel: all claimed that they were the best, the most important, the most useful, the favourite.

Green said: *Clearly I am the most important. I am the sign of life and of hope. I was chosen for grass, trees, leaves – without me, all animals would die. Look over the countryside and you will see that I am in the majority.*

Blue interrupted: *You only think about the earth, but consider the sky and the sea. It is the water that is the basis of life and drawn up by the clouds from the deep sea. The sky gives space and peace and serenity. Without my peace, you would all be nothing.*

Yellow chuckled: *You are all so serious. I bring laughter, gaiety, and warmth into the world. The sun is yellow, the moon is yellow, the stars are yellow. Every time you look at a sunflower, the whole world starts to smile. Without me there would be no fun.*

Orange started next to blow her trumpet: *I am the colour of health and strength. I may be scarce, but I am precious for I serve the needs of human life. I carry the most important vitamins. Think of carrots, pumpkins, oranges, mangoes, and paw paws. I don't hang around all the time, but when I fill the sky at sunrise or sunset, my beauty is so striking that no one gives another thought to any of you.*

Red could stand it no longer. He shouted out: *I am the ruler of all of you. I am blood – life's blood! I am the colour of danger and of bravery. I am willing to fight for a cause. I bring fire into the blood. Without me, the earth would be as empty as the moon. I am the colour of passion and of love, the red rose, the poinsettia and the poppy.*

Purple rose up to his full height. He was very tall and spoke with great pomp: *I am the colour of royalty and power. Kings, chiefs, and bishops have always chosen me for I am the sign of authority and wisdom. People do not question me – they listen and obey.*

Finally, Indigo spoke, much more quietly than all the others. *You hardly notice me, but without me you all become superficial. I represent thought and reflection, twilight and deep water. You need me for balance and contrast, for prayer and inner peace.*

And so the colours went on boasting, each convinced of his or her own superiority. Their quarrelling became louder and louder. Suddenly there was a startling flash of bright lightning: thunder rolled and boomed. Rain started to pour down relentlessly. The colours crouched down in fear, drawing close to one another for comfort. In the midst of the clamour, Rain began to speak: *You foolish colours, fighting amongst yourselves, each trying to dominate the rest. Don't you know that you were each made for a special purpose, unique and different? Join hands with one another and come to me.*

Doing as they were told, the colours joined hands. The Rain continued: *From now on, when it rains, each of you will stretch across the sky in a great bow of colour as a reminder that you can all live in peace. The rainbow is a sign of hope for tomorrow.*

And so, whenever a good rain washes the world, and a rainbow appears in the sky, let us remember to appreciate one another.

Author unknown

In our study of the meaning of colours, which follows, we consider the dualistic nature of how humans think by citing each colour's positive and negative attributes: the negative represents the things you can focus on to transform aspects in your life. Contact with colour can lead to instant transformation because it has an energetic vibration as do you: it cuts through your resistance like nothing else and enables you to: connect to what is playing out in your everyday reality as well as forgotten issues that created beliefs and certain emotions. It helps you to master your emotions, giving you the ability to see multiple perspectives; to harness your energy and creativity; to develop your personal autonomy and authentic power; and to get totally clear on your guiding vision for a meaningful life. Resembling an enhanced psychometric test in one way, working with colour using our *KK Systems™* will help you shift states. The coloured oils we provide work on the cellular memory of an individual to help stabilise and restore balance by lifting the hidden patterns that lie in the subconscious and bringing them into

45

conscious awareness. These patterns may have been inherited through the family gene pool or taken on as beliefs or fears since being born.

In the rest of this chapter, we give you the background for our system. We examine the importance of colour and its psychological evolution, along with its relationship to psychometric testing. We then consider Spiral Dynamics because it is an organisational development tool, it is based on colour and on levels of consciousness, and offers an entry into the study of colour. After that we illustrate how colour fits into the area of leadership development by showing how our work builds on Laloux's thinking. As much of our work focuses on raising consciousness, we then take a look at the role of the chakras in all this, as well as exploring dimensions of reality. The final part of this chapter is dedicated to looking at the Colour Mirrors System on which all our work is founded.

The Origins of Colour Therapy

Imagine a world without colour – everything would be black, white or grey. How would that make you feel? You just have to recall a rainy winter's day to see how easy it is to slip into feeling bleak. Interestingly, the HSBC building at Canary Wharf in London has a predominantly grey interior with the odd bit of red; many working there have commented on how that has dulled their mood on entering the building. Those aware of the impact of the lack of colour do all that they can to arrange business meetings elsewhere. Colour has more impact on you than you may realise.

In the psychology of colour, there are three primary colours – red, yellow and blue. These refer to physical, mental and emotional states of being. Green and violet represent balance and harmony; when they are added, the spiritual elements are then included.

We are trained colour therapists and as such, we use colour to balance energy wherever it is lacking in the human physical body, whether that is in the physical, emotional, mental or spiritual realm. We work out where there is an imbalance based on the selection of colours that you pick. At any given time, the colours you select will provide insight into your emotions, your unconscious fears, your desires and potential, your health and wellbeing. Colours, like the human body, have an energetic vibration; after a session working with colour, your vibration is higher and you usually feel lighter. Colour is a tool for shifting stagnant or negative energy. Leaders are often unconsciously drawn to colour without necessarily recognising that they are looking for a shift in their outer or inner reality. Colour therapists are able to make sense and give meaning to what is happening as we connect people deeply to their emotions to help them find the answers and the deeper meaning to the situations they find themselves in.

This is possible because colour is working at an energetic level; we help individuals to see their unconscious (and sometimes conscious) patterns of behaviour. This process gives them full access to the soul's intuitive wisdom to make sense of the past and present so that they can move forward in a way that is more aligned to their true nature. Taking the time to access this is actually uncommon sense in a world where the emphasis is on doing and collecting more material objects at the cost of feeling. At the organisation level, this is played out in the way that executives keep themselves busy and then when they start to slow down and create white space, they experience a fear of both freedom and having time to reflect. It brings up a degree of uncertainty, so execs revert to their conditioned way of being, and either stick to the rules or create rules to ensure there is certainty, rather than trusting that order will emerge out of chaos.

Whilst individuals have their own particular relationship with colour, it is also true that some colours have universal meanings. It is widely accepted that warmth, comfort, anger and hostility emanate from the warm colours, whilst calmness of the mind, sadness and authority are associated with cool colours.

Modern research[2] into colour shows that blue-coloured street lights lead to a reduction in crime in built-up areas, and putting prisoners in a pink environment calms them down and leads to less violence. If you own a yellow car, you will be involved in fewer accidents, whereas there is a higher likelihood of an accident if you drive a red car.

Colour therapy has existed for centuries. It has roots in Ayurveda, a form of Indian medicine practised for thousands of years and has links with ancient Egyptian culture and Chinese healing. In traditional Chinese medicine, for example, each organ is associated with a specific colour. Ancient Egyptians built solariums (sun rooms) that could be fitted with coloured panes of glass. The sun would shine through and flood the client with colour. The Greeks also identified colour with universal harmony. Belief in the divine healing property of colour pervades all ancient symbolism.

Newton and Goethe

To appreciate the origins of Western colour therapy, we need to look at Newton and Goethe, who contributed much to our understanding of colour today. Newton formulated the first theory of colour and he, along with Locke, is the co-founder of empiricism, which influenced the development of the mechanical paradigm in leadership development theory.

Goethe also worked with colour. His work *Theory of Colour* is not really a theory; he used this work to refute aspects of Newton's theory and through his book, provided a catalogue of how colour can be perceived in a wide variety of circumstances.

When Goethe first began his studies of light, he claimed that Newton was completely wrong.[3] From our current perspective, Newton's approach is left-brained and analytical, whilst Goethe's is right-brained and artistic.[4]

In their experiments, Goethe and Newton differentiate between the warm colours (red, orange and yellow) and the cool colours (violet, indigo and blue). But what of green? Green is a blend of a warm colour (yellow) and a cool colour (blue). Picture a rainbow and you will notice that green is also the bridge between the warm colour palette (red, orange and yellow) and the cool colour palette (blue, indigo and violet).

Complementary Colours, the Role of Magenta and the Psychology of Colour

Goethe's work is also very important because, through the colour wheel he produced, he introduced our Western civilisation to complementary colours. He wrote: *The chromatic circle... [is] arranged in a general way according to the natural order... for the colours diametrically opposed to each other in this diagram are those which reciprocally evoke each other in the eye. Thus, yellow demands violet; orange [demands] blue; red [demands] green; and vice versa: thus ... all intermediate gradations reciprocally evoke each other; the simpler colour demanding the compound, and vice versa.*

Goethe completed his colour wheel by recognising the importance of magenta. His approach led him to recognise the essential role of magenta in a complete colour circle – a role that it still has in all modern colour systems today. Goethe was the first to discover magenta and he named it. Comprising of 2 parts red and 1 part blue, this tertiary colour lies "hidden" between red and violet. Therefore magenta is both the end and the beginning of the Light Spectrum and as such, it contains or holds all the other colours including white light. We could refer to it as the Alpha and Omega of the spectrum of colour and as such is referred to as the entry point into colour.

Goethe also believed that colours had an aesthetic quality. In other words, he attributed meaning to each of the colours on his colour wheel. We suggest that he was the founder of the modern day psychology of colour.

Psychometric Testing

Humanity's natural curiosity for understanding personality has existed for aeons. We all want to understand different people and their particular strengths and needs. Behavioural and personality models have been used by philosophers, leaders and managers for hundreds, and in some cases thousands, of years as an aid to understanding, explaining, and managing communications and relationships. The popularisation began with Socrates and Aristotle, and has continued right through to modern times where behavioural and personality models are widely used in organisations, especially in psychometric testing.

Many psychometric assessments are based on the concept of the four humours that suggest that all bodily fluids influence human temperaments and there is a balance of black bile, phlegm, yellow bile and blood in the body; whilst we know little about its origins, the Greek physician Hippocrates (c. 460 – c. 370 BC) developed it into a medical theory. In AD 190, Galen of Pergamon classified the four temperaments as recognisable human states corresponding to the four elements and the four seasons. These were sanguine (extroverted, fun-loving, optimistic, impulsive, social – air and spring), choleric (extroverted, hot-tempered, strong-willed, quick-thinking – fire and summer), melancholic (introverted, analytical, private – earth and winter), and phlegmatic (relaxed, peaceful, easy going – water and autumn).

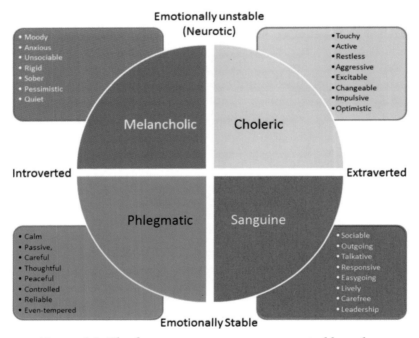

Figure 1.1: The four temperaments represented by colour

As you can see, colour is implicit within the four temperaments: it builds on them and adds a further dimension. Although there are a few well-known tests based on colour such as the Strengths Deployment Inventory and Insights Discovery, we feel our system goes way beyond what they offer. *The KK Systems*™ go much deeper.

Our approach is based on a more substantive set of colours to reflect the complexity of human nature.[5] In Chapters 3-5, we explore the seven fundamental colours (Violet to Red) including Magenta, which acts as the entry point into colour. Three chapters follow these; they focus on the next set of colours, which act as the transitionals, or the bridge, between the core colours and legend territory.

We build on the work that was started in the 20th century by Clare Graves with his depiction of the evolution of humanity using colour. Spiral Dynamics, based on Graves' work and created by two of his students, is a psychological approach that offers insights into people's world views and how these shape values and drive behaviour. Put simply, it is a study of consciousness and how that has evolved through history. It is such a comprehensive system that we devote an entire section of this chapter to explore it further.

Spiral Dynamics – Evolution of a Consciousness

Don Beck and Christopher Cowan's book, *Spiral Dynamics: Mastering Values, Leadership and Change,* presents, in fascinating detail, a spiral developmental model of world views. Beck and Cowan call these patterns of thinking vMemes (values-attracting meta-memes). vMemes can be thought of as broad orienting paradigms – schemas by which we interpret the world. There are eight levels of vMemes. Each vMeme leads to certain beliefs, social groupings, motivation patterns, organisational dynamics, and goals. It is worth noting that the descriptors beyond yellow are less well defined. This is because one of the limitations of Spiral Dynamics as a system is that it originates from yellow vMeme thinking and so it was hard to find concrete language to define the states of higher consciousness – turquoise and coral.

In the rest of this section, we present the first and second tier vMemes as described in Beck and Cowan's book. What are tiers? We use the European Union as an example to elaborate on them. Going back to the EU's formation in colour terms, this was a blue response, in Spiral Dynamics' definitions, to the red chaos created by World War II and the need to take increased control to facilitate the greater good. As the EU has evolved over decades, many countries have sought membership for their own economic ends, which is an orange phenomenon. At the same time there has been

51

an increased desire for a "federal" Europe, with a free movement of individuals and a reduction in sovereignty of individual nation states. These trends have green attributes with orange undertones. There is limited second-tier level consciousness, which is an understanding of the interdependency that Europe could have. It also helps to explain what was happening at a sub-conscious level when people in the UK voted no to remaining part of the EU.

Each vMeme has emerged historically in response to the needs of new, and more complex, life conditions. The rest of this section outlines the key characteristics of each vMeme.

<u>First Tier</u>

1. **Beige**: At this level we are highly instinctive – this includes the fight or flight instinct – and tribal people living a simpler existence can often hear, see and smell better; they can sense changes in the weather. 100,000 years ago, our ancestors lived at this level permanently as they needed to focus on survival. It is not very prevalent today, although everyone can and does access this state at times, especially under extreme stress. If there is a catastrophic collapse of society, those that survive will probably be the ones that can access their beige instinct. The only time we see beige today is in the mentally ill, street people, those with senility or late-stage Alzheimer's: it represents about 0.1% of world population.

2. **Purple**: This colour emerged when clans had to come together and form tribes because the space available was reduced due to the Ice Age. Blood bonds are strong as group identity outweighs the concept of the individual. Superstitions and magic characterise these people who are cyclic in outlook. Rituals, traditions, and symbols are very important for these groups; they tend to use voodoo, lucky charms and superstitions: they represent 10% of world population, one per cent of power.

3. **Red**: The law of the jungle lives in red and it's characterised by despotic monarchs corrupted by power; it is the exploitation of unskilled labour and is epitomised by the sectarian nature of the Southern states under slavery. This is where individual ego appears for the first time. In this world, there is a strict division

of haves and have-nots. The root assumption is that people are lazy and must be forced to work. Red is hedonistic, focused on the pursuit of pleasure with little thought of the personal or wider consequences. Today, this behaviour is evident in urban gang warfare. There is a lot of aggression in red. We see this behaviour in toddler tantrums, rebellious teens, mercenaries and many celebrities: it represents 20% of world population, five per cent of power.

4. **Blue**: This colour emerged as a way of dealing with the excesses of red as it appealed to a higher order. There is a sense of purpose expressed in blue and a need for order that leads people to obey authority; to feel guilty when not conforming to group norms; and to serve the greater good through self-sacrifice. Industrial economies tend to run according to blue principles. Blue is good for building empires. In corporates, orange management slip into blue when under stress to take control. There are strict hierarchies. Boy and Girl Scouts, Puritan America, religious fundamentalism, the Inquisition and Victorian Britain are examples of this: it represents 40% of world population, 30% of power.

5. **Orange**: This evolved when the restrictive, oppressive nature of blue became overwhelming; we then had the Enlightenment accompanied by self-determination and ambition. It is the dominant vMeme in the US today. It embraces rational thinking; individuals in orange calculate what is to their personal advantage and motivations are largely economic. This is the work culture that is motivated by extrinsic rewards such as perks, bonuses, and money rather than intrinsic ones such as a sense of belonging to the group. The root assumption is: competition improves productivity and fosters growth. There is a strong need for autonomy that can lead to the manipulation of the environment. Orange mainly leads to a free market economy and multi-party democracy. Examples of orange are the cosmetics industry, Hong Kong and the World Trade Organisation: it represents 30% of world population, 50% of power.

6. **Green**: This colour appears when there is a realisation that "winning" and material success lack meaning. The focus is on community and personal growth, equality, environmental

concerns. Green is fiercely anti-hierarchical. There is a desire to belong, so being liked becomes more important than competitive advantage. Value is placed on openness and trust, and there is a fear of rejection and disapproval. Greens can get lost in the search for consensus and find it hard to be decisive. This inward-looking nature is what was witnessed in the Occupy Movement and is why it imploded: it did not want to go back to the competitive individualism of orange. Greenpeace is probably the clearest example of green thinking along with Rogerian counselling and animal rights: it represents 10% of world population although this rises to 30% in Europe, 15% of power.

Second Tier

The second tier operates at a much higher frequency than the first tier. In the first tier everything is a fear-driven response to reality, whereas in the second tier the key motivator is love. One of the biggest shifts is the capacity to hold multiple perspectives about everything. The other main difference is that from the second tier you can choose to inhabit any of the previous vMemes if that serves you, whereas in the first tier, each new vMeme is a reaction to the excesses of the previous vMeme. For example, green is a response to the material excesses of orange. The blue need for order comes out of the chaos created by gangland warfare in red.

7. **Yellow**: Systems thinking originated in yellow and its driver is to come up with solutions for all the issues that greens can see. The emphasis is on learning for its own sake and the integration of complex systems. Yellow organisations embrace change because they like a challenge and because they view change as a necessary part of the process. There is an interest in how parts interact to create a greater whole. The systems' perspective of infinite diversity in multiple combinations is honoured and seen as contributing something valuable to the whole. Yellow likes dealing with ideas. It is also ecologically oriented, but in a subdued, behind the scenes way compared to green. Yellow thinkers often work on the periphery of organisations, quietly fine-tuning situations and procedures: they are not interested in status. Hawking's *Brief History of Time*, chaos theory and

Wired epitomise yellow: it represents one per cent of world population, five per cent of power.

8. **Turquoise**: It is holistic and focused on a global holism/ integralism, attuned to the delicate balance of interlocking life forces. As Don Beck said, *Yellow is left brain with feelings, whilst Turquoise is right brain with data.* The two vMemes complement each other and work alongside each other. Work must be meaningful and it enables the overall health of life. Feelings and information are experienced together, enhancing both. Turquoise leaders are conscious of energy fields, holographic links in all walks of work and life, and have the urge to use collective human intelligence to work on large-scale problems without sacrificing individuality. Examples are: Gaia hypothesis, Ken Wilber, Teilhard de Chardin, David Bohm, Gandhi's idea of pluralistic harmony: it represents one per cent of world population, one per cent of power. This colour is still emerging and is not very influential yet.

In the original work by Clare Graves, the system stopped at turquoise. The remaining two colours, coral and teal, came from different sources and were added much later. This is part of the reason why the descriptions are not as detailed.

9. **Coral:** Here, what the Buddhists call a 'bodhisattva' emerges; this is a person who works tirelessly to bring out the inherent possibilities in others. The following quotation we've chosen reflects coral very well:

Conflicts will diminish as our global, universal, spiritual, and cosmic awareness increase. By far the greatest contribution to peace an individual can make is to become a global, universal, and cosmic being ~ Robert Muller (Amity House, 1986) *A Planet of Hope*

10. **Teal**: This colour is even less well known. It has gained much more recognition recently through Laloux's work.

One way of understanding teal is to look at Margaret Wheatley's[6] work on change. She is the president emerita and co-founder of the Berkana Institute. In an article[7] she co-wrote in 2006, Wheatley states that the world doesn't change one person at a time; rather it changes as networks of relationships form among people who discover they share a common cause and vision of what is possible. In the article she goes on to suggest that networks grow and transform into active working communities of practice and that change happens through emergence[8] in the following way:

Stage 1 is the development of networks which is defined as *the only form of organisation used by living systems on this planet. These networks result from self-organisation, where individuals or species recognise their interdependence and organise in ways that support the diversity and viability of all.*

Stage 2 is the evolution into communities of practice. *In a community of practice, the focus extends beyond the needs of the group. There is an intentional commitment to advance the field of practice, and to share those discoveries with a wider audience. They make their resources and knowledge available to anyone, especially those doing related work.*

Wheatley argues that change can happen very quickly in communities of practice. Good ideas move rapidly among members and new knowledge and practices are implemented quickly.

Stage 3 involves *the sudden appearance of a system that has real power and influence. Pioneering efforts that hovered at the periphery suddenly become the norm.* Critics can become lead supporters. Pioneers become leaders in their field and are considered wisdom keepers for their particular issue.

Wheatley states that emergence is the key for bringing about the sustainable change that so many now long for. She adds that there is a progression from networks to communities of practice to systems of influence.

Coral can therefore be defined as a "community of practice," similar to turquoise, but not as cohesive, and in teal, this community becomes a "system of influence." That influence is exerted in both visible and invisible ways, on every imaginable scale and some scales beyond imagining!

The above has been an introduction to the distinctions between turquoise, coral and teal, and we will now explore Laloux's work for a deeper understanding of what teal is all about.

Laloux's Work and Thinking about Colour

Frédéric Laloux[9] describes the historical development of human organisations. He builds on Spiral Dynamics by identifying what he sees as the three most important colours influencing the shape of organisation development today. They are red > orange > green – all First Tier vMemes. He then focuses on the new vMeme, teal, based on Ken Wilber's Integral Theory, that is not part of the original Second Tier and suggests that its characteristics are now present in some forward-thinking organisations today.

Whilst we agree that there is definitely evidence of an awakening in both society and business that can be defined as an evolving consciousness, we go further in our approach. We suggest that to fully connect with and understand teal, one first needs to integrate other aspects. We have added in a set of transitional colours – Turquoise, Coral, Pale Gold, Olive Green and Amber – that act as a bridge to move from Green to Teal. We explore these in detail in chapters 6 to 8.

Laloux defines the characteristics of the colours magenta and amber differently from the way we do. For him, magenta is akin to purple in Spiral Dynamics and refers to societies that were prevalent 100,000 years ago where superstition dominated and the elders held authority. For him, amber relates to society as it was 1,000 years ago with the principle characteristics of formal hierarchies where command control and the stick held sway. Whilst we would agree that amber concerns preservation and ancestral connection, we see Amber as being far more instrumental in shaping today's construct because it recognises individual talents and gifts. Moreover, we see Amber as fundamental to the emergence of Teal. It helps to ground this high vibrational energy.

We see Magenta playing the role of the catalyst within the colour wheel, much as Goethe did. For us, it acts as the gateway between the seven fundamental colours and the transitional colours; it also has the quality of transformation in that it is the starting point of any journey into deeper self-awareness when using colour. Think of Magenta as that inner voice that presents a subtle nudge, more often than not in midlife, about the meaning of it all and the search for the higher self. We define it as the soul waking up and as the search for personal mastery. The nudge may be for some people the loss of a child, the bereavement of a beloved parent, the desire to travel, a move to the southern hemisphere or just a feeling of restlessness and a sense of lack of fulfilment even when everything looks good on the outside. As our values surface more because we get challenged, a way can be opened into connection with the soul.[10] Everyone gets the nudge, but it is their choice whether they respond to it.

Why is there a greater range of colours in The KK Systems™?

Our view is that organisational development is not linear. In line with systems thinking, we know that it is more complex than that. In our work, we frequently find "ghosts" in the system. Ghosts are old archetypal energies that have a lasting impact on organisations. For example, many CEOs feel unable to put their own stamp and authority on an organisation's culture due to the legacy left by the previous incumbents that have occupied the CEO chair. This pulls their focus back into the past rather than maintaining a present or future orientation. This is often an unconscious act that sabotages their efforts.

We differ from Laloux, in that, in *The KK Systems™*, we facilitate leadership transformation and cultural shifts through the use of colour. Our premise is based on the functioning of the right brain – how people feel affects how they perform. This is still one of the most overlooked concepts in business today. We agree with Laloux that Amber is a preserving force with a link to ancestral lines, but it is from this point on that the paths of Spiral Dynamics and *The KK Systems™* separate. Amber for us is a transitional colour, which sits between the root and sacral chakras. It builds self-belief and self-reliance – essential ingredients in purposeful work.

Even though Laloux claims that his model is not linear and that there is room to evolve consciousness in a particular colour, he places great emphasis on teal being the end state which we should aim for. This is too narrow, as it could lead adherents of colour to believe that increasing one's level of consciousness comes from moving upwards through the colour system. For us it is far more complex than that, as leaders can model aspects of many colours at the same time and can only evolve through accessing the transitional colours.

Further to this, Laloux's premise is based on a mental construct which emphasises the importance of intellectual thought, whilst our work is based on an emotional construct where the importance of feeling is the focus. In other words, we operate out of a feminine perspective, whereas Laloux and many organisational development theorists operate from a masculine perspective. We also know that when you create from the mental plane, there is greater tendency to judge the outcome and the gap feels too big to close – creating your dream becomes an almost impossible, Sisyphean task. Within each and every person lie hopes and fears about their future possibilities; and, in our work with leaders and organisations, we focus on what is possible because we know that that is the start of the journey to better outcomes that are more aligned to company values.

The Role of Chakras[11]

As previously stated, chakras exist just off the body and they govern our psychological properties. There are seven principle chakras and they all contribute to our sense of wellbeing. They start at the sole of the foot and go up to above the crown of the head and are linked by meridian lines. When our chakras are balanced, we are functioning optimally in terms of our health, mental faculties and inspiration.

The three lower body chakras start with the root chakra. Using the seven primary colours, the colour for the root chakra is red and, like the basic needs in Maslow's hierarchy of needs, it governs our feelings relating to safety and security. The second lower body chakra is the sacral chakra, represented by the colour orange – it governs our emotions and creativity. The third lower body chakra is the solar plexus, represented by the colour yellow; when it is fully open we feel in control, and have high self-esteem – it is the power centre. The heart chakra, represented by green, is the transformation point between the upper three chakras and the lower three. You will not be surprised to hear that it is related to love, kindness and compassion and it is involved with harmonious relationships. The fifth upper body chakra, represented by blue, relates to the throat and involves self-expression and communication. The sixth chakra, represented by indigo, is referred to as the third eye and it enables us to access greater levels of insight and intuition; if imbalanced it will lead to rigidity of thinking and manipulation of others to get one's needs met. Finally there is the seventh – the crown chakra – represented by violet, which relates to wisdom and spirituality.

Traditional and Enlightened Chakras

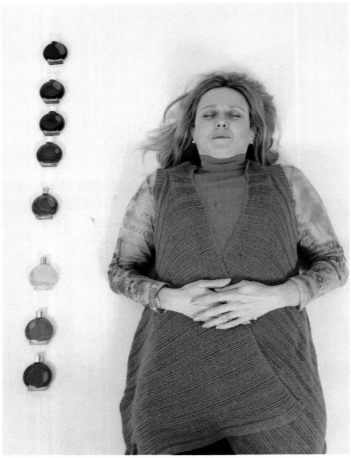

Figure 1.2: A body with each of the seven main chakras represented by a bottle

When you have activated and balanced your chakras, apart from enjoying improved health, it is quite usual to experience psychic or spiritual perceptions and visions. Your awakened chakras will rewire your neural circuitry, awakening parts of your brain that have previously been dormant.

When you take your personal development seriously and work on it regularly, you start to have quantum leaps in your understanding, which lead to greater self-realisation. In colour terms, this is represented by the enlightened chakras; the traditional chakra colours (the fundamentals) still relate to the majority of information that humans hold. We will now consider each chakra from an individual and organisational perspective.

In chakra 1 (the Red/ Red bottle), which represents the root chakra, we move from Red (not feeling safe/ dependent) to Enlightened Red (Clear/ Clear). This represents a move from the survival state to the thriving state. The underlying tenet is recognition that we are not separate and that we have the ability to let go of our judgements. From an organisational perspective, this chakra represents the systems, processes and infrastructure of a business. Examples are: how we collect cash, how we distribute products and how we manage a customer complaint. Slick processes help facilitate the flow of energy, which enables the cash to flow. In Enlightened Red there tends to be a surplus of cash; focus tends to be on how to be more conscious around money and give back, not because the organisation has to, but because it wants to.

In chakra 2 (Orange/ Orange), which represents the sacral chakra, we move from Orange to Enlightened Orange (Orange/ Rose Pink). This shows that love has the possibility to heal all. Underpinning this aspect is the learning that life does not need to be about a series of sacrifices; we can start to live with greater compassion and we can have more fun. In organisational terms, because there is a sense of belonging, co-operation is valued along with teamwork. In Enlightened Orange organisations, there is an emotional connectivity and intelligence which leads people to go the extra mile for each other.

In chakra 3 (Yellow/ Yellow), which represents the solar plexus chakra, we move from Yellow to Enlightened Yellow (Gold). This represents a move from fear to authentic power. The spiritual tenet holds that, by being in power we can let go of the need for control. In Gold organisations, there is a degree of healthy conflict as there is an understanding that questioning, far from being disruptive, can actually lead to increased wisdom. This is only possible because trust is widespread within the organisation.

In chakra 4 (Green/ Green), which represents the heart chakra, we move from Green to Enlightened Green (Lilac/ Pink) which is about changing the emphasis on the quality of love so it moves from being conditional to something much more expansive. Nurturing and appreciating all that we ourselves are becoming, rather than focusing on others, can facilitate this. This represents the heartbeat of an organisation and those doing Enlightened Green are the ultimate learning organisations.

In chakra 5 (Blue/ Blue), which represents the throat chakra, we move from Blue to Enlightened Blue (Blue Violet/ Blue Violet). This represents an ability to be more considered in our responses, which have become more closely aligned with our true feelings and higher self. There is the awareness that every moment, whatever it brings, is perfect. At an organisational level, there is an honesty and transparency in the communication processes. The degree to which leaders can model feelings depends on the extent to which an organisation is in Enlightened Blue. There is recognition of communication that involves understanding and inclusivity and which facilitates shared exchanges and provides opportunities to ask for the ideas, opinions and feelings of all those involved. All of this builds a cohesive culture.

In chakra 6 (Indigo/ Indigo), which represents the third eye chakra, we move from Indigo to Enlightened Indigo (Gold/ Clear). This is about living with an expansive vision, which brings our life and our work together as one. In this enlightened space, we hold the faith and can trust the process, knowing we can create. At an organisational level, the degree to which organisations are future-focused, shape trends and opportunities, and the degree to which they are comfortable with change and innovation depend on whether they are Indigo or Enlightened Indigo. The more leaders can model optimism in times of ambiguity and uncertainty, the more fear dissipates.

In chakra 7 (Violet/ Violet), which represents the crown, we move from Violet to Enlightened Violet (Clear/ Lilac). This represents moving from worshipping something outside of ourselves, to recognition of the divine within us. From an organisational perspective, it is moving from doing things "right," to sensing the evolutionary purpose of an organisation and creating from that point.

As you can probably now appreciate, some of the shifts required to move from the existing to the enlightened chakras are massive; and because of this, there are transitional colours in place, serving as stepping stones. The transitionals serve as openings to higher states of consciousness once the lessons of each colour have been integrated. We devote three chapters (6-8) to these and their significance.

Dimensions and Consciousness

Each one of us experiences the world in different ways because we are operating in different dimensional realities; our private, individual experience is dependent on the lens through which we see reality. As mentioned earlier, our level of perception is based on a combination of the conscious mind, the thoughts we have (around 10% for the average individual) and our unconscious mind, which is a collection based on all our past experiences, belief patterns, memories, meta-programmes and social conditioning (around 90%). We are subjected to images and programmed paradigms during childhood; up to age seven, the mind is largely a sponge absorbing everything in its environment and accepting it as the norm without question. Therefore, we have a tendency to delete, distort and generalise because of the power of our unconscious mind over the conscious. This is one of the key reasons why *The KK Systems*™ focuses on the importance of emotions.

The unconscious mind is the feeling mind which cannot tell the difference between what is real and what is imagined. This is one of the reasons why visualisation techniques have become such a powerful construct in business and sport. As Goethe said: *Before you can do something, you must first be something.* Self-belief is a crucial ingredient to gaining self-confidence. Self-belief comes by holding the right thoughts in your mind about where you want to go and who you want to be.

If you think of humans as computers, we are both the hardware and the software. Then comes the question: who is doing the programming? The answer: we are, in that we are learning to master the interior space – learning how to be disciplined around our intentions and thoughts and choosing how we wish to feel. Conscious intention involves building beliefs by modelling successful people in action and becoming more of who we want to be.

The more time we spend on the inside, the greater the opportunity we have to observe our thought patterns in action and to start to question the truth of them. The more self-reflection we do, the clearer we get around the vision for our life and work. We find ourselves at cause rather than effect.

The journey of personal mastery begins as we recognise ourselves as *spiritual beings having a human experience* (Teilhard de Chardin) and that at a base level we are nothing more than colour, light, and frequency. Your physical body exists in a third-dimensional realm and the auric field that surrounds you is a fourth-dimensional energy field. The former is a state of being and the latter is a state of potential being.

In fourth-dimensional reality, we come to understand that time is not, in fact, linear – it is fluid – and the observer of the universe actually becomes the participator. This has now been verified by quantum physics. Consciousness has many layers and many dimensions of reality.

When life is lived mainly from the third dimension, it is experienced as a reactionary environment. We see ourselves as entities, separate from one another, and life happens to us. In one way, it is like living in a two-room bungalow. In another way, there is a past, a present and a future and life unfolds in a linear direction. In the fourth and fifth dimensions, we observe, choose and act on our intentions, thus liberating ourselves from the dramas of life. These dimensions offer us full creative potential where we co-create and construct our reality consciously. In this reality we have present-time focus and, returning to our bungalow metaphor, at this level, the house has now expanded to become a two-tier construct. We achieve a lot more with a lot less effort and renew our energy whilst doing so. In terms of leadership, leaders who are playing it small and always asking for validation live in the two-room bungalow, and leaders who are quietly confident with their own internal locus of control stand firmly in two-tier constructs.

Our connections with dimensions and consciousness can be seen as doorways leading to an expanded awareness of perception and self. It starts when we get curious and ask, *Surely there must be more to life than this?* From that moment on, answers come and we start on a path that goes deeper into the nature of spirituality: we begin to see the interconnection of all things.

The Colour Mirrors System

Colour Mirrors was developed by Melissie Jolly in late 2001. Implicit in the name is what the system does: it offers the opportunity to reflect back to us the reality around us through the lens of colour to raise our self-awareness and build our emotional and social intelligence. Jolly teaches us that just as we don't wash the mirror when our face is dirty, so we need to look at our own issues which are being reflected back to us and sort them out. She has a background in psychology and fine art, and during her training, she noticed that people changed when working with certain colours. This awareness was enhanced in that she has both synaesthesia, which enables her to see the patterns within colours, and heightened psychic sensitivity, which has given rise to incredible creativity.

We all have an electromagnetic, or auric, field around us. Through Kirlian photography, we can see our energy fields as colour, based on the frequencies of the energy. When a person is presented with an array of colours, like a set of coloured oils or a rack of clothes, they are immediately drawn to the colours in their own auric field. So through the filter of your own energy field you choose the colours you need. Everything you have ever experienced is represented in your auric field in colour.

Colour Mirrors incorporates the Hindu teaching of chakras with energy centres in the body divided into a rainbow. The rainbow goes from red at the base, which is the lowest frequency, to violet at the crown, which is the highest frequency.

Complementary Colours

In his work on archetypes, Jung articulates the importance of the shadow self in understanding the whole person. Building on what Jung discovered, Colour Mirrors uses complementary colours to help explain the unconscious, more hidden, elements of the individual.

Every colour has a complementary colour except for Pink (which is really a higher vibration of Red), and Silver. Silver has a seventh-dimensional quality about it, which means it is elusive in nature and is giving us a glimpse of what is possible. It doesn't want to be pinned down and, if you do that, like quicksilver, it will lose its luminosity.

We deal with the complementaries here because it is helpful to keep in mind that they represent the unconscious or hidden parts of yourself that you are not ready to acknowledge yet. By having an awareness of them, you get a greater sense of what's going on for you. Below is a table of all complementaries and underneath that, we detail what they mean and what the spiritual laws are in relation to each colour.

Red - Green
Orange - Blue
Yellow - Violet
Indigo - Gold
Pale Gold - Platinum
Olive Green - Magenta
Turquoise - Coral
Amber - Teal

Red is results oriented and when we apply the spiritual law of non-judgement we are able to see a higher perspective about the actions we take and the results that we get. Also, by taking responsibility and moving out of blame and victimhood, we accept that on every level we create the conditions that produce the results we get. In its extreme in overt red organisations, we see an efficient machine with an obsession for bottom line results. Whilst the results are achieved, employees burn out without a compelling vision, and an over-emphasis on the rules creates a compliant culture. Over time these become bureaucratic, monolithic structures which prompt the best talent to leave in search of greater freedom.

Green is an empowering culture and the spiritual law of self-love focuses on learning about the importance of clear boundaries and space creation as a platform for mutual respect; this leads to effective collaboration. As the focus turns from doing to being and recognising others, the drive for competition falls away as people see the value that each brings to the whole. For organisations, whilst they will still scan the external environment, they become less concerned about their competitors and more focused on their own progress.

Orange is a relationship builder and creativity, and the spiritual law concerns learning the importance of forgiveness. When we allow ourselves to let go of old hurts, we feel a sense of belonging to the whole. For organisations, if this doesn't happen, the whole organisational focus is on getting even rather than getting on. There is simply a collection of fiefdoms within a firm rather than a cohesive whole.

Blue is consultative, traditional and inspirational; spiritually it is about learning that everything is perfect when we refrain from judging our experiences. This allows us to stay in neutrality and recognise that there is no failure – only feedback. When we can adopt this mindset and model it, we learn from our mistakes and are less likely to repeat them. We also become a great deal more conscious in modelling integrity. An organisation, then, will have a reputation that delivers beyond its promise.

Yellow is mental agility, focus and precision; its spiritual perspective is about full empowerment. This is only possible when you let go of your ego and share the power and information. For organisations, this means thought leadership, archiving and dissemination of information to stay ahead, add value and look credible.

Violet represents ethics and integrity and values-led leadership. The spiritual law operates from the concept of service to all. In organisations, there is alignment to the vision and it is possible to unite all voices to the whole because the organisation is operating from a sense of a higher purpose.

Indigo is a change agent. This is where there is real appreciation that humans at their core are far more than an intellectual construct. There is understanding that they are motivated by their hopes and dreams. At an organisation level, there needs to be greater appreciation of the collective unconscious in operation. This is the focus of our work because we, as authors, know that all voices in the system need to feel deeply understood by being seen and heard in order to align with the collective vision of the organisation as a whole. When positive feeling states are built, then anything is possible.

The following transitional colours offer a way forward for leaders and organisations to shift from a focus on systems and processes to wholeness and authentic expression. They embrace a new way of being with a greater emphasis on relationship intelligence and a fundamental understanding that the bridge between the knowledge age and the information age is investment in people.

Gold is authenticity and Pale Gold is the futuristic alchemist, whilst platinum is personal mastery or, the void. An example of the void is the idea that as leaders, the more we trust ourselves and allow ourselves to be led by our intuition because of an inner knowing that we will know what to say in the moment, the more we are operating from the void. Olive Green represents feminine leadership and collaboration with a dash of social responsibility, whereas Magenta is about being more and doing less. Turquoise is being in flow and intuitive intelligence, whilst Coral offers us interdependence and wisdom. And finally, Amber is contemplative and affirms our sense of self-belief, so we can embody our fullest potential. Moving from the interior state of Amber to the exterior state of being, we actualise Teal. Teal represents unity consciousness and, sitting as it does between Turquoise, the higher heart and the throat chakra, the emphasis is on speaking with love.

The KK Systems™

The KK Systems™ has evolved out of our work both as colour therapists using the Colour Mirrors system and as coaches in the transformational change arena. We felt that there was a need for a bespoke colour system that focused specifically on business and facilitated courageous conversations which would enable leaders to question their unconscious assumptions, norms and behaviours that reinforce the status quo. We see an organisation as a human, living system which is either evolving or blocked. As the saying goes, *The fish rots from the head.* The intention behind our work is to scramble leaders' conscious minds so that they stop thinking their responses and start feeling them instead. We take leaders from separation and a place of fear into uncertainty so that they can appreciate what unity can bring. Another way of looking at this is that the third-dimensional reality is just a construct that confines and limits individuals' potential. Through our work, leaders get to experience and discover higher dimensional realities.

In foundational colour terms we start with Violet which represents the crown chakra; in organisational terms this typifies business ethics and values; and Indigo which represents the third eye chakra – in organisational terms this delivers the vision. This approach leads to breakthrough territory for sustainable results. However, it takes time, and this is often not acceptable in the busy "do, do" culture of today's business world.

The first four of our eight principles

We have eight principles that underpin *The KK Systems™* and our work. Our first principle is that as a leader, you need to take responsibility and recognise that you are always at choice. This tenet is based on a fundamental belief that we are co-creating our reality all the time.

When leaders have accepted the concept of personal responsibility then they are able to begin to appreciate the difference that others bring. This is held within the second of our principles, value and recognise others in their wholeness. Diversity brings richness and infinite possibilities.

Today, there is recognition that there is a desire to move away from a directive leadership style to a more authentic coaching style of leadership. In our terms, this means staying true as leaders to your highest values with no need for external validation. In other words, the third principle: let go of control and allow all the voices of the system to be heard. True power then becomes authentic.

The more inner-directed leaders become, the more they can allow themselves to be in flow as there is no fear of failure. At this point leaders are better able to embrace the next of our principles: Know yourself; nurture your growth, set appropriate boundaries. People don't need fixing. They just need to feel seen, heard, and understood. Leaders can only be inspiring to themselves and others when they have accepted and integrated more of their whole selves. This is only possible is when they connect to their emotions – recall those whose words have inspired you the most and you will know this to be true. So our fifth principle is: to inspire others you must first inspire yourself. Integrate your head and your heart to build cohesion.

Our remaining four principles

As leaders become more conscious about what drives them and how they get in their own way, they realise they need to unlearn conditioned thinking and reconnect to who they really are at their essence. We advocate to leaders the importance of using their intuition because it is a competitive advantage in a world where everyone is drowning in data. This gives rise to the next of our principles: Feel it ... think it ... do it ... just be it.

As leaders start to recognise that they are enough, they cease to look outside themselves. They embrace the tenet of non-attachment and focus on raising their vibration so they feel joy. The seventh principle is: non-attachment to outcomes.... follow your bliss, do what you love, bring your innate gifts and uniqueness into the world. All of these ideas can be summed up in the final principle: there is no certainty with transformational change except what is created from the inside.

We explained earlier that our work goes beyond models, and what that means in concrete terms is that we ask organisations to learn to live with ambiguity without reverting to the rules that they followed before. Our work is about promoting white space to enable leaders the time to reflect, thereby giving everyone the freedom to interpret the organisation's values as they see fit. We know that allowing autonomy will enable mastery and assure productivity. It is the embodiment of trust, yet so many leaders struggle with trusting both self and others and taking full responsibility for their reality creation. The old paradigm enforced the hierarchy and levels of decision-making that cascaded down the lines. In new paradigm businesses, every voice in the system is recognised, which means there needs to be a greater degree of consultation based on appreciative inquiry. Listening to the feelings behind the words brings a greater degree of collaboration. As a starting point, the middle way may involve establishing a common framework to which all are aligned. What stops this from happening?

We have observed three patterns common to all leaders: avoidance, distraction and addiction. As you read this, consider what your primary pattern is and that all these patterns are driven by fearful states of being. Avoidance builds a defensive and fearful way of being and closes leaders off from deep connection with their people. Avoidance represents a reluctance to change or to be open to new ways of thinking and being. Distraction is often the most common trap, as we've all been conditioned to believe that if we are on the go 24/7 we're at least doing something productive and taking action and being seen to be more effective. The technological impact only serves to exacerbate this worrying trend. Distraction often shows up in other ways such as the need to absorb and question things purely from the logical intellectual sense. Addiction is evident in the addictive behaviours regarding wealth and power across big business, and society at large. Addictive behaviour is never sustainable: it will always, at some point, unravel any leader who abuses authority.

In Chapter 1, we explained why our world is at a crisis point and why the next 20 years are critical in determining the fate of the human race. In this chapter what we have explored with you is our take on leadership and how to transform the culture of organisations. Sustainable change in organisations only comes when leaders transform themselves from the inside out. We also explained the origins and the kinaesthetic power of colour with examples of the different dimensions of consciousness at which colour operates. We have also introduced the idea of how colour can start to shift states. The outcomes (the hardware) can only change when you have cleaned the software. Colour helps to raise awareness and unlearn learnt behaviour because it enables you to release old, stagnant energy by processing out the negative feelings that lie behind it. It works at a very deep level because it delivers integration and full embodiment.

We have also used this chapter to give you a sense of the origins of colour therapy and the interplay between colour and psychology, in particular regarding psychometric tests. Many psychometric tests owe their foundations to Jungian principles: in particular the concept of the seen and the unseen. We have also taken the opportunity to explain how we differentiate our offering and why there is such a need for it today. And now we invite you to come on a journey with us and see how you can be more of that leader you were born to be.

Notes

1. Self-leadership means you have a developed sense of who you are, what you can do, and where you are going coupled with the ability to influence your communication, emotions and behaviors on the way to getting there.

2. Some research looking into short wavelength light (blue) has demonstrated that it is a potentially effective treatment for seasonal affective disorder (a seasonal type of depression; see for instance, Glickman, et al., 2006)

3. The primary Newtonian experiment is the pinhole and prism, where the colours are spread out on a surface a small distance away.

4. The primary Goethean experiment involves the prism, where light and dark boundaries are seen, showing in one orientation the "warm" colours (red, orange, yellow) spreading out over the light area and in the other orientation, the "cool" colours (violet, indigo, blue) spreading out over the dark area.

5. Recognising the need to show the complexity of human nature, we illustrate this through the use of Colour Mirrors, a system based on 13 colours as opposed to the existing tests based on three to four colours, maximum. We find these to be overly simplistic and do not reflect the true richness that makes up human behaviour.

6. Margaret Wheatley received her doctorate in Organizational Behavior and Change from Harvard University, and a Masters in Media Ecology from New York University. She has written nine books; her most famous is *Leadership and the New Science* which has been translated into 18 languages.

7. Margaret Wheatley and Deborah Frieze (2006) *Using Emergence to Take Social Innovations to Scale*

8. Emergence – as a theory in change management, emergence infers that change is largely fluid and emerging, that it is all pervasive and continuous and often cyclical and iterative.

9. Frédéric Laloux (Nelson Parker, 2014) *Reinventing Organizations*

10. If you want to understand the connection between values and identity further, we recommend Robert Dilts' model about the logical levels of change.

11. The Sanskrit word 'chakra' literally translates to wheel or disk. There are seven main chakras which align along the spine starting from the base of the spine to the crown of the head. These swirling wheels of energy correspond to massive nerve centres within the body and they organise our psychological, emotional and spiritual ways of being. This invisible energy is vital life force which keeps us vibrant, healthy and alive.

The Fundamentals (CHAPTERS 3-5)

Figure 2.0 The Fundamentals

Overview

In this section of the book, we go deeper with our approach, *The KK Systems™*. Each of the following sections is dedicated to a particular colour starting with the foundational colour and going onto its enlightened version. The structure we outline below is for the foundational colours only. The enlightened colours, which operate at a higher frequency, have a looser structure in line with their higher vibration. Each subsection starts with a link to a model or a concept from the wider environment that will help you to grasp the essential characteristics of the colour. We identify the positive and negative traits of each particular colour to give you a sense of it and then we present the characteristics of leaders that operate in this space. We also cite, in most sections, specific examples of the culture and structure of the corresponding organisations that represent aspects of that colour. However, this approach comes with a health warning in that it emphasises the extreme polarities and dualistic nature of each colour. In reality, the less labelling that is done, the easier it is to see the underlying patterns and become aware of the transformational effect.

It is human nature to identify with colours and even to have a favourite colour. This can change during one's lifetime which can reflect changes on a more profound level. When humans understand the colours of their soul pattern, then deeper transformation is possible. However, too much identification with a particular colour is not advised because humans are inherently complex and when they operate to the fullest of their capacities they can access a range of colours. We are therefore not talking about stepping through Red and then each of the colours through to Magenta to achieve self-actualisation, because evolution is not linear – it is more of a spiral.

So that you will have an image of the spiral-like tendency of evolution, the first of the three chapters in this section will start at the very top (Magenta/ Magenta) and work down. Magenta is the gateway to the whole system so it is not treated in the same way as the colours that follow. You will notice that whilst the subheadings are the same for each colour, the type of information given is different. This is because the energy vibration is more arcane the higher you are in the body and language is sometimes inadequate to explain what is happening there. Spiritual energy is above the head. What that also means is that there are fewer examples of leaders operating at the higher frequencies: they are rare indeed at this time!

Personal Breakthroughs with Colour

Before we dive into the fundamental colours, we'll explore how colour is applicable to you and your life. The reason that you can expect breakthroughs working with colour is because colour approaches change in a much more right-brained way than any other system. You discover how to be a new paradigm leader because you can't overthink colour – you have to let go of your intellect and thereby move from doing to being. This is a fundamental principle of being a new paradigm leader. We are not saying that action is unimportant, but we are saying that it is secondary to who you want to be and what your values are. Whilst the majority of leaders follow a Do, Have, Be modus operandi, our philosophy for breakthrough results comes from a Know, Be, Do, Have model which starts with a full appreciation of the value of intuitive intelligence.

Simply holding the colour bottles and/ or spraying specific spritzers can lead to fundamental shifts as new insights and connections are made that were previously unconscious. Working with colour puts us firmly in touch with our intuition. The transformation goes deeper if you meditate and then bathe in the colours that you feel drawn to. This is because colour tells a story and the story the colour tells gives the reason for the challenge. When we know why something exists, we can release it. This is very important if it feels that an injustice has been done, because in those situations, it is very difficult not to feel victimised and then be stuck with the issue. Much of our unconscious response in this regard is to play the role of persecutor or rescuer, which merely serves to reinforce the separation game. When this is happening, board members can fall out with one another and there is a degree of churn as the power struggle continues. This is because men, who make up the majority of the boardroom, often tend to go on the attack when their emotions are triggered. All of this is compounded because the expression of feeling is difficult for many and frequently disallowed in the boardroom. Colour can serve to access those feelings, explore and understand them and enable the process of healing and growing, even without words.

The kinds of breakthroughs you will experience as a leader are: you will be able to manage whatever work throws at you because working with colour can increase your resilience and help you to see how powerful you really are in a fuller, more congruent and authentic way of being. It can therefore help you to stop the inner conflicts and the self-sabotaging, clear up any feelings of imposter syndrome and help you to spend more time in your adult self. The degree to which you know and understand yourself through working with colour will shape and inform all your relationships in life and business and make you a phenomenal connector. In business terms, what you will see modelled is an energy and momentum that goes way beyond the concept of team working, as interest in both organisational politics and power for its own sake wains. Fear dissipates and every voice is heard, because there is a desire to collaborate and create a better whole.

In our work, we have seen numerous examples and born witness to the transformation of many seemingly powerful leaders of both genders who felt far from that and who felt the need to hide aspects of themselves in order to fit in and deliver what was required. At the point of entry into organisational systems, a lot of ego is present, which is what leads to toxic behaviours and negative emotions. Working with colour enables leaders to see that FEAR is just a false expectation appearing real and therefore that they no longer need protection from their egos.

Chapter 3:

Magenta, then Violet, Indigo and Blue

Magenta: the Entry Point into the System

Figure 2.1 The Entry Point into Colour (Magenta/ Magenta)

Dan Siegel,[1] author of *Mindsight*, wrote: *The human psyche [is] defined as the soul, the intellect, and the mind.* The turning points that humans experience are often triggered by an appreciation of how much more there is to life, and by the soul yearning for an awakening. As they reach higher levels of consciousness, people are recognising that we are multi-dimensional beings that have had to switch off our full capacities in order to exist in this earthbound, third-dimensional plane.

A key trait in Magenta is the ability to notice and observe what is happening beyond the obvious. Magenta leaders start to yearn for something else. Whilst they may have a lot of success, they feel an emptiness that sits behind it – a hole that needs filling. The materialistic pursuit of the achievement-oriented leader just doesn't deliver fully anymore. It's from this place of questioning that the journey inward begins.

These leaders are also observing what needs healing, what is missing and what brings them joy. In *The Happiness Project*, Gretchen Rubin, whilst riding a city bus, asked herself, *What do I want from life?* She discovered through her thoughts that she wanted to be happy and began to realise she had spent no time pondering happiness. It was in that given moment, the now moment of Magenta, that she decided to dedicate a year to her happiness project. This led to a thriving industry and fascination with the search for happiness. It is no longer a blog or a book: it is actually a movement where groups have been formed for people to discuss their own happiness projects.

One of the reasons it is difficult to define specific positive or negative characteristics of Magenta is that it acts as the catalyst that brings about the transformation. The ground rules for any form of major shift show how people approach change differently.[2] The key is that it is Magenta that will nudge people into action as explored in more detail in the previous chapter.

Magenta: the Century of Awakening

Figure 2.2 Awakening Bottle (Magenta/ Copper)

There is a strong link between numerology and colour. The initial 36 bottles that Jolly created for the Colour Mirrors System were numbered 1-36. The 21st century started in 2000 and so from a colour perspective, we are in the century of awakening as the 20 bottle is Magenta over Copper and represents the deepening awareness of the needs of the higher self. Since ancient times the term 'awakening' has been used as a metaphor that points to the transformation of the human consciousness.

Awakening is an awareness that you no longer need to create stories to make sense of your reality – you just need to find your whole self and let it unfold in the moment. It is knowing that all is perfectly imperfect and that you are enough just as you are. Magenta acts as a blueprint for the colours that follow. It is a process in creation and evolution. The mantra for Magenta is "Wake up, the only time is now."

It is possible to stop struggling in this life and find joy and fulfilment in this moment now. The ultimate expression of this is that the search, which used to be on the outside, goes within, as the search for the whole self becomes the created self. The essence of this journey is about healing the inner child.

In Magenta, if you start to question the old ways of working, then you find inspirational answers that unfold in an inspired way to deliver alternative models and processes that lead to a better way of being.

Positive characteristics of Magenta

From a business perspective, a positive Magenta leader would be John Fullerton. He has been the founder and lead at Capital Institute since 2010: a provocative new voice, grounded in a deep understanding of mainstream finance. He represents the positive characteristics of Magenta because he is healing the inequities and injustices caused by the abuse of power displayed within the banking fraternity, which led ultimately to the 2008 financial crisis. Capital Institute is redefining wealth and re-imagining finance in service of something bigger. Fullerton has taken an in-depth knowledge and 18 years of background in banking to become a thought leader in the new economy; he promotes equitable development and shared wellbeing. He was part of JP Morgan when 9/11 occurred and following that, he developed a deep interest in systemic failures. This led him to develop new models for societal regeneration.

From an organisational perspective, Magenta contains holism and the concept of the organisation as a living system. This is the appreciation that all parts of the system that make up the organisation are in intimate interconnection and the whole is worth more than the sum of the parts. This is a necessary pre-condition for any organisation to understand its evolutionary purpose.

A great example of an organisation that models these positive characteristics in Magenta is Patagonia. In 2013, Patagonia had an anti-Black Friday campaign called "Buy less, wear for longer". They supported it with a film called *Worn Wear* in which eight people shared their thoughts on how to treat the clothing we wear in the most sustainable way.

Negative Characteristics of Magenta

It's not companies that change: it's people. So why is there resistance? Magenta works on the limbic system: the seat of emotional memories. If in your reptilian brain there is a particular memory of an event that caused pain or of an action that did not work, at the moment you experience something similar in your present, your reptilian brain will put the brakes on the change in order to protect you. Emotions hold much more sway over humans than logic. Here's the rub. If you resist and push away the change, then it will come back in a stronger form. Magenta is willing you to move in the direction of your fullest potential and yet, often it is fear that holds you back. The longer you resist, the ruder the awakening. In resistance, the focus is constantly on the doing. In organisations where there has been little focus on personal development, there can be quite a lot of resistance to leadership coaching initiatives. In client organisations, there have been leaders that have refused to answer emails and get involved in coaching initiatives because initially they felt fairly very cynical about them. It took skilful handling to bring them on board.

In the negative polarity of Magenta, leaders experience burnout from overdoing. We can see this through the fascination with "busyitis" in the corporate world today. What leads to overdoing? Is it technology or is it a disassociation from feelings and connection? Many people choose not to connect with their emotions or even define themselves as "objective personalities" – there is a fear of emotions, so overdoing becomes the substitute for feeling because it ... feels easier. This focus on overdoing acts as a salve to the prick on people's conscience as they convince themselves that they are doing the right thing; in reality, however, it is only a temporary fix.

Fred Goodwin, boss of the Royal Bank of Scotland (RBS), represents an archetypal negative Magenta leader. He got a reputation for paring costs – so much so he got the nickname "Fred the Shred". Twenty takeovers helped him transform RBS and then he overstretched himself in 2007 by leading the $100 billion takeover of ABN Amro. RBS' capital reserves were stretched to the limit and the UK Government had to bail out the bank which created losses of £28 billion. This is a classic example of overdoing. Many blame Fred's actions for contributing to the 2008 financial crisis arguing that he was motivated by greed. He personifies the current predicament we face, which is that the current capitalist system has created extreme inequality. This inequality has become a threat to the very system that is creating it. It has led to increasing levels of separation, isolation and desperation, which are all qualities associated with negative Magenta.

Magenta is about connecting to your essence, because Magenta reminds us of the language of the soul. The following story represents the gift of Magenta if we allow ourselves the space and the freedom to slow down and tune in a while.

The Parable for Magenta
The Song of your Soul

The little girl asked her grandmother, *Grandma, what is life?*

Grandmother replied, *Life is a song, my love.*

Oh, said the little girl. *I want to learn that song.*

Everyone has their own song, my dear, replied Grandmother. *I cannot teach you yours, you have to discover it yourself.*

Oh Grandma, how can I find my song? asked the little girl.

Grandmother called her close and whispered in her ear, *You need to listen, my love – to the flowers and the trees, to the river and the rain, to the night and the stars and, more than all else, to your heart – and your song will come to you.*

Whether it is to find your own sense of purpose as a leader, or to connect to your organisation's evolutionary purpose, you need to learn how to stop doing, so that you can appreciate all the opportunities that are right in front of you.

There is no enlightened Magenta because it sits above the initial seven colours and links them to the transitionals. Magenta is the starting point of any journey through colour – after every breakthrough and shift, there is a return to Magenta to start the process again.

Introducing the Top Three Chakra Colours: Violet, Indigo and Blue

Working with colour is not a linear process. To help you anchor this concept, this section starts with Violet, which is at the top and works down to Blue.

When we are inspired, we are typically employing and accessing these higher chakra points. Inspiring thoughts typically create higher impulses and warm, fuzzy feelings in the body that feel great. That is the higher frequency energy that's available when it is mixed with the energy of the heart. Violet is more refined in quality than its complementary colour Yellow. When we feel good and we have inspired thoughts, the quality of our work improves and success breeds success. The more we operate from this place, the more we receive.

The key is to trust your heart to move where your unique talents can flourish. This old world will really spin when work becomes a joyous expression of the soul ~ Al Sacharov.[3]

Violet

Figure 2.3 Crown Chakra (Violet/ Violet)

Picture any typical English village and what you will generally see are the pub and the church at the heart of it. English people love this sense of continuity, ancestry and heritage and laud their culture over newer ones by suggesting that they lack depth because they are not so steeped in history and tradition. Whilst it is important to have a sense of where you have come from, it can hold you back from breakthrough territory. If we look further at the meaning of these symbols we can see that allegiance to either the Church or a drink equates to giving power away. And yet if you look a little closer, you can see that the attraction of the Church or a drink comes from a desire for community and union.

Religious faith can be so mesmerising. It offers people a way to make sense of life and loss. The Church was also seen to offer a way to grow, through penitence and sacrifice. Christian values are woven into the fabric of Western society, as can be seen in the idea that it is better to give than receive. In the past, the institution of the Church tapped into people's fascination with the unknown and unseen, providing rituals and rites of passage to give life meaning and give individuals the hope to carry on.

So what does this have to do with the colour Violet? The essence of Violet is an inborn desire to want to make a difference and serve others. It is imbued with the sense of wanting to leave a legacy and the need for meaning-making and improving life for all, through social justice and building community. Violet leaders are full of conviction and highly principled.

Violet leaders are driven by a clear sense of purpose, have an impeccable track record and a strong moral compass. They want to allow the full expression of spirit in their conscious desire to do right in the world and in business even to the extent that they will whistle blow and out companies with shoddy practices.

Positive Traits of Violet

The essence of Violet is a caretaker who looks after all aspects of society, recognising that there are those that have and those that are in need, and that all are deserving despite their inequality. Violet leaders embody sincerity and humility. They engender trust and are the archetypal servant leaders.[4] Servant leadership is a philosophy and a set of practices concerned with enriching the lives of individuals, building better organisations and creating a more just and caring world. It is less to do with the accumulation and exercise of power and more to do with acting with integrity.

Violet leaders have strong values, champion social causes and rally people behind their mission. They champion social reform. A good example is Joseph Rowntree who, as a businessman, wanted to improve the quality of life for his employees. For modern day reference we would like to cite the social entrepreneur, Daniel Flynn, who heads up Thank You. Thank You is a social enterprise whose purpose is to end global poverty. They give away 100% of their profits into four main product ranges – water, body care, food and baby stuff.

Culturally, there is a philanthropic feel to the ethos of Violet organisations and they often assert a coaching and mentoring style of leadership. And this is now reflected in the "Millennials," who increasingly search for values-led organisations to work for. The mantra for Violet is "Just do the right thing."

Negative Traits of Violet

From a business perspective, negative Violet leaders operate from the principle of "we know better." When they cannot find an outlet for their strong ethical stance, they have a tendency to rant and rave about the injustice of it all.

Violet has an aspirational quality about it; however, when others pay no heed to Violet leaders' ideas, they can end up being rather pompous and start to blame and judge others for the lack of outcome. They believe that they know best and the reason others don't act is because they don't get it. Their convictions are so strong that they can often alienate others, who see them as opinionated or even fanatical about their beliefs. There is an almost religious zeal about the beliefs of Violet leaders that can make them appear to be preachy. There is a certain intensity about them which can leave those who attempt to connect with them feeling exhausted.

For those running this pattern, life can feel like hard work and very restrictive. As principled people, Violet leaders have a clear-cut definition of what is right and wrong and they often have tunnel vision, meaning they will pursue an issue until they get justice whatever the personal cost. *The Gamechangers*, a BBC docudrama, documents the controversy over *Grand Theft Auto*, a violent video game series made by Rockstar Games. An evangelical attorney, Jack Thompson, tries to get the series banned by claiming that it had detrimental psychological side effects on young minds. Fuelled by his own sense of self-righteousness and having little respect for due process, not only does Thompson fail to stop Rockstar Games: he ends up getting disbarred. Thompson is an example of what can happen to a negatively driven Violet lawyer when he overplays his strengths.

Parable for Violet

The parable below focuses on another aspect of Violet leadership and that is the effect of powerful intentions. In recent times there have been a slew of books that focus on conscious leadership.

The Rabbi's Gift

This parable was made famous by M. Scott Peck, but was originally told by Francis Dorff. We have quoted it in full here because it is not well known.

"A famous monastery had fallen on hard times. Formerly, its many buildings were filled with young monks, but now it was all but deserted. People no longer came there to be nourished by prayer, and only a handful of old monks shuffled through the cloisters, serving God with heavy hearts. On the edge of the monastery woods, an old rabbi had built a little hut. He would come there, from time to time, to fast and pray. No one ever spoke with him, but whenever he appeared, the word would be passed from monk to monk: *The rabbi walks in the woods.* And, for as long as he was there, the monks would feel sustained by his prayerful presence.

One day the abbot decided to visit the rabbi and open his heavy heart to him. So, after the morning Eucharist, he set out through the woods. As he approached the hut, the abbot saw the rabbi standing in the doorway, as if he had been awaiting the abbot's arrival, his arms outstretched in welcome. They embraced like long-lost brothers. The two entered the hut where, in the middle of the room, stood a wooden table with the scriptures open on it. They sat for a moment in the presence of the Book.

Then the rabbi began to weep. The abbot could not contain himself. He covered his face with his hands and began to cry too. For the first time in his life, he cried his heart out. The two men sat there like lost children, filling the hut with their shared pain and tears. But soon the tears ceased and all was quiet. The rabbi lifted his head. *You and your brothers are serving God with heavy hearts*, he said. *You have come to ask a teaching of me. I will give you a teaching, but you can repeat it only once. After that, no one must ever say it aloud again.*

The rabbi looked straight at the abbot and said, *The Messiah is among you.* For a while, all was silent. The rabbi said, *Now you must go.*

The abbot left without a word and did not once look back. The next morning, he called his monks together in the chapter room. He told them he had received a teaching from the rabbi who walks in the woods and that the teaching was never again to be spoken aloud. Then he looked at the group of assembled brothers and said, *The rabbi said that one of us is the Messiah.*

The monks were startled by this saying and asked themselves: *What could it mean? Is Brother John the Messiah? Or Brother Matthew or Brother Thomas? Am I the Messiah? What could all this mean*? They were all deeply puzzled by the rabbi's teaching, but no one ever mentioned it again. As time went by, the monks began to treat one another with a new and very special reverence. A gentle, warm-hearted concern began to grow among them which was hard to describe but easy to notice. They began to live with each other as people who had finally found the 'special something' they were looking for.

When visitors came to the monastery, they found themselves deeply moved by the life of these monks. Word spread, and before long, people were coming from far and wide to be nourished by the prayerful life of the monks and to experience the loving reverence in which they held each other. Soon, other young men were asking, once again, to become a part of the community, and the community grew and prospered. In those days, the rabbi no longer walked in the woods. His hut had fallen into ruins. Yet somehow, the old monks who had taken his teaching to heart still felt sustained by his wise and prayerful presence."

This parable shows that to build a vibrant community, there needs to be both self-respect and respect for one another. Violet leaders are imbued with this and they are often described as having a great deal of integrity.

Enlightened Violet (Lilac)

In order to understand the dynamics of an Enlightened Violet leader, we cite the work of David Hawkins, a well-known psychiatrist and physician, who commenced research in 1975 on the kinesiological response to truth and falsehood.

Figure 2.4 Enlightened Violet Chakra (Clear/ Lilac)

Kinesiology, in case you are unfamiliar with it, is essentially the study of muscles and their movement. It first received scientific attention through the work of Dr George Goodheart, who found that at a level below conceptual consciousness, the body ultimately "knows" what is good and bad for it; through muscle testing he was able to signal this. A classic example is the weakening of indicator muscles in the presence of a chemical sweetener; those same muscles strengthen in the presence of a healthy natural supplement. Later on, Dr John Diamond began refining this speciality into a new discipline that he called behavioural kinesiology. He discovered that indicator muscles would strengthen or weaken in the presence of negative emotional and intellectual stimuli as well as physical stimuli. Positive statements such as *I love you* will test strong. Negative statements such as *I hate you* will test weak. And what is so fascinating about Diamond's research is the uniformity of his subjects' responses. They were predictable, repeatable and universal even where no rational link existed between stimulus and response.

David Hawkins realised that this research indicated some form of communal consciousness – a database of collective consciousness available to all. All this points to what is now generally stated in terms of quantum physics, that is, that the human mind, at a basic primal level, is linked with a universal energy field and therefore knows far more than it realises it knows.

Through 20 years of research and millions of calibrations on thousands of subjects, Hawkins was able to analyse the full spectrum of consciousness. This anatomy of consciousness gives us a profile of the entire human condition, allowing us to comprehensively analyse the emotional and spiritual development of individuals, groups and societies, and man as a whole.

From observation of the mind's thoughts and motivations, we now know that our every thought impacts on our consciousness and view of reality. Our every thought and action leave an enduring trace forever in the universe. The human mind is like a computer terminal connected to a massive database of information. We all have access to this database. Hawkins sees it as the realm of the genius mind because a certain energetic frequency is necessary to be able to tune into what's available: and that is spiritual intelligence and power.[5]

The likes of Jesus Christ's and Lord Buddha's energy fields would have calibrated at levels of 1,000 and above on Hawkins' map, and truly spiritual states of unconditional love begin at a calibrated level of 500.

Hawkins' work offers us an in-depth insight into what authentic power looks like, as opposed to power that is driven by force. Force always creates resistance because fear sits behind it, whilst authentic power builds flow, as it is a power based on the expression of love. Hawkins used Ghandi as an example of this.

At the end of British colonialism in India, the position of the British Empire was calibrated below the critical level of 200 on the scale of consciousness. The motivation of Mahatma Ghandi calibrated at 700, very near the top range of normal human consciousness. Ghandi achieved India's independence because his position was one of great and authentic power and when force meets power, force is always eventually defeated.

There are numerous examples throughout history where society tried to treat social problems by passing regulations and by engaging in warfare, market manipulation and prohibition. All these reactions are expressions of force, which, due to recurring persistence of these problems, often simply get stronger. A very present example is the current rise of extreme Islamic fundamentalism – a direct result of the "war on terror" response and the destabilisation of the Middle East through prolonged warfare. The conditions of social conflict will not disappear until the underlying causes have been fully exposed and healed. When we choose empathy and compassion with the complete absence of judgement, we start to heal past divisions, attitudes, emotions and behaviours characteristic of the energy fields below 200.

As Violet leaders find that place of inner peace and clarity in Enlightened Violet, they begin to understand the impact their self has on others. They accept that it is as it is. The following parable illustrates this well.

Parable for Enlightened Violet
Two Pots: a Perfect Tale of Imperfection!

Many years ago over in China there was a lovely man who lived in a mountain village. Because he loved his beautiful wife and family so much he got up early every morning and he would pick up two pots with one of those sticks you put across your shoulders, and he would walk for a mile and a half to a river to get clean water.

This meant his family could get washed and have breakfast. It put a smile on his face seeing them happy. He did this every single morning. He would walk down the same path, collect the water in the pots, turn around, and then come back the same route every single morning. Being a perfectionist and loving order, he never varied his route.

However, this story is really about the two pots. One day the pots got talking to each other. One of the pots unfortunately had a few cracks in it and the water would leak out of it, so by the time the lovely man got back home from the river, it was only a third full. The other pot was nice and shiny and brand new and had no cracks in it and didn't leak.

During the conversation, the perfect pot said to the cracked pot, *You seem to be a bit down at the moment – what is wrong?* The cracked pot was really upset and, given the opportunity, poured out his sadness. *I feel really humbled in your presence and admire how perfect you are. Every day we come back and you are still full of water. I'm only a third full if I'm lucky and I feel really upset about that. I feel like I'm broken and not providing as much value as you do.*

The perfect pot thought about this for a while and replied, *Well, have you ever noticed that on the way down there are some really beautiful flowers on one side of the path, and have you noticed that the man picks some of the flowers for his wife every single morning? He brings the flowers back and he puts them in a vase and his wife comes down to breakfast and sees the flowers and is really happy.*

The cracked pot said, Y*es, I have noticed this, and it makes me feel great seeing the smile on his wife's face every morning. The perfect pot then asked, And have you noticed that the flowers only grow on one side of the path?* The cracked pot replied, *Yes, it is strange, isn't it?* The perfect pot then asked, *Why do you think that is?*

The cracked pot thought about this for a little while and realised that what was happening was that, as they were walking back from collecting the water every single day, the cracked pot was watering the flowers and making the flowers beautiful. On the other side of the path where the pot did not leak there was no water and no flowers grew.

Very few get to a point where they can accept all of who they are and see that everything – the highs and the lows – in their life's journey has been for a reason. To get to that point, we have to increase our faith in, and our connection with, Source[6] and let go of the need to know and control everything. We must find inner peace in order to become the compassionate leaders in society at large. All this requires an awareness of our spiritual selves; this can bring about greater ease and joy with what is unfolding right now, rather than hanging on to past hurts and resentments.

Enlightened Violet, therefore, has in many regards a futuristic quality which has not yet emerged – only a few shining lights have appeared throughout history. From our point of view, it is so very much needed and aspirational at this time. The mantra for Enlightened Violet is "My word is my bond."

Indigo

Figure 2.5 Third Eye Chakra (Indigo/ Indigo)

Hundreds of years ago, a traveller walking through the countryside came across three men who were laying bricks. He asked the first man what he was doing. *I am laying bricks,* was the reply.

I am earning money, said the second.

The third man – well, he was different. He stood up straight, lifted his head upwards and with a big beaming smile, he said, *I am building a cathedral and one day when it is finished I will show my children around it and explain my role in creating this magnificent structure.*

The third man has Indigo consciousness. He can see the bigger picture behind the activity he is engaged in, whereas the first two men are more prosaic and see what they are doing as a task or a means to an end.

In our introduction, we talked about some of the adverse effects of technology and the increase of social media. Indigos tend to focus on the possibilities that these two aspects can bring. Piera Gelardi, Creative Director and Co-founder of Refinery29, an award winning

94

lifestyle digital media company, has predicted that social media will lead to a shared consciousness and a version of telepathic communication in the next 15 years.

It is easier to understand the world of Indigos if we look at how society is shifting. A major reframe is taking place around the role of reason and rationality. Today in the workplace there is greater allowance for introspection and self-reflection, exemplified by the popularity of Mindfulness. There is increased recognition that empathy gives us a conduit to understand what we feel and a way to conceptualise our emotions. In 2007, *Time Magazine* selected Frans de Waal, a biologist at Emory University, as one of the world's most influential people. He states that feeling and acting with empathy for others is as automatic as aggression. De Waal points to modern psychology and neuroscience research, which support the concept that *Empathy is an automated response over which we have limited control.* He highlights the fact that many animals survive, not by eliminating each other or by keeping everything for themselves, but by cooperating and sharing. Indigo leaders are naturally empathetic and if, as de Waal's research suggests, empathy is the glue which binds society together, then, this is what enables Indigo leaders to make intuitive leaps. The clearer the energy field is, the less triggered they become by stuff that is happening around them. There is more mental white space, and this enables both more room for introspection and access to greater intuition.

Positive Characteristics of Indigo

A key characteristic of an Indigo leader is their keen, intuitive intelligence. Richard Barrett, author of *The New Leadership Paradigm*, provides the principle characteristics of intuitive decision-making:

1. Awareness is expanded through a shift in one's sense of identity/ consciousness.
2. Judgement is suspended. No meaning making takes place, either subconsciously or consciously.
3. The mind is empty. Thoughts, beliefs and agendas are suspended.
4. The mind is free to make a deep dive into the mind-space of the collective unconscious and emerge with a deep sense of knowing.

5. The thoughts that arise reflect wisdom and align with one's most deeply held values.

Indigo leaders make intuition-based decisions, where there is no focus on the past or the future. They accept what is without judgement. Their ability to make intuitive decisions arises out of their presence in the current moment. When they are values-led, they make decisions based on the positive feelings they want to experience now and in the future. Many, however, tend to make decisions based on their beliefs which come from their past experiences, which tend to be self-limiting.

It's this absence of judgement in Indigo that creates the perfect conditions to allow their minds to tap into the collective mind-space; their intuition informs them of what wants or needs to emerge. The ability to do this consistently increases as the shift from ego-mind to higher self (soul) takes place.

Indigo leaders have great independence of spirit and are often the mavericks in their organisations. They get away with this because they are plugged into their environments. They are those early adopters/ pioneers who foresee and act on new trends and opportunities. With a visionary nature, they are classic storytellers and they inspire the hearts and minds of others in their organisation.

An Indigo Leader: Steve Jobs

We suspect you won't be surprised that we have chosen Steve Jobs as the archetypal Indigo leader. Right from the early days, he followed his own path. He never made it to university, but that did not deter him from finding his own way. He stands out as the ultimate example of inventiveness and the application of intuition in business. A future pacer, he was a visionary who could see what others could not see. And he was so much a visionary that, even though he left Apple, he was asked to come back and be CEO a few years later. He is quoted as saying:

Have the courage to follow your heart and intuition. They somehow already know what you truly want to become. Everything else is secondary.

96

Indigo organisations are constantly evolving and clear about the need to align with an expansive vision and they are constantly checking the cultural climate for threats and opportunities. They thrive on change and being able to influence the direction of trends. Their ability to think laterally and divergently is what gives them edge to come up with completely new ideas - they are often the trendsetters.

Google: an Indigo Organisation

Google is an Indigo organisation. Since its IPO in 2004, its shares have soared over 900%. The company's success stems from its continuous innovation. Google keeps the pipeline of innovation open by tapping its employees and letting ideas percolate up. In 2013 their innovative practices included:

1. Google Cafés, which are designed to encourage interactions between employees within and across teams and spark conversation about work as well as play.
2. Direct emails to any of the company's leaders.
3. Google Moderator, a management tool designed by Google's engineers. When people have tech talks or company-wide meetings, it lets anyone ask a question and then people can vote for the questions that they'd like answered. Through Moderator, people can discover existing ideas, questions or suggestions, vote for ideas, questions or suggestions, see the aggregate votes to date, and then create a new series asking for ideas organised by topic, event or meeting. Google Moderator came out of Google's infamous 20% projects.

The company allows its engineers to spend 20% of their work week on projects that interest them, which enables the organisation to tap into the many talents of its employees.

It is hardly surprising, therefore, that Google was also one of the first companies to fully embrace the adoption of Mindfulness practices within the organisation. The company could see the benefit they would bring to the bottom line.

Negative Traits of Indigo

Indigo leaders are highly empathic. Often they soak up environmental toxicity and they are quite likely to become ill if subjected to large levels of it.

Whilst the enquiring nature of Indigos has a positive intention, it can often get them into trouble and they can be ostracised from the pack. Archetypally, they are the mavericks and lone wolves in business who struggle to be team players. They prize autonomy over most things and can be very challenging to manage especially if they feel they are being told what to do. They have very little respect for processes, and in larger organisations this means that they can be seen as disrupters.

They have fabulous insights on a personal level but they can struggle to unpack them for others' benefit. This is because they are foreseeing things that are not part of the common understanding and they are often misunderstood or mocked. They are difficult to work with because they are always changing the rules to suit their circumstances with little regard for how that makes others feel. They can set up situations in such a way that it looks like the other party is at fault. When they feel isolated, they use manipulation to get their own agenda accepted. As they understand the underlying motivations of others, they make formidable adversaries because they sense their opponents' weak points and play on them mercilessly if threatened.

Part of the nature of Indigos is to find their own path. This means that they rarely appreciate being given a way forward, and in extreme situations will become aggressive and seem obstinate, stubborn, and inflexible.

An Indigo business in a downward spiral is extremely divisive, political and challenging, isolating and alienating. There will be lots of suppositions, lots of back room deals and the aim of the game will be to set people up to fail.

Parable for Indigo
Jonathan Livingstone Seagull

Jonathan Livingston Seagull mirrors many of the qualities of Indigo leaders in that they are always searching for higher levels of existence. They are not frightened of being unconventional and doing their own thing as a means to finding them.

Jonathan befriends a wise gull, Chiang, who expands his mind beyond his previous learning, teaching him how to move instantaneously to anywhere in the universe. Chiang explains that the secret is to begin by knowing that you have already arrived. This epitomises the leadership style of Indigos, which is very much about following flights of fantasy within the imagination that lead to great innovative leaps that they then bring back and share with their organisation. The mantra for Indigo is "Be, Know, Do."

Enlightened Indigo (Gold/ Clear)

Figure 2.6 Enlightened Indigo Chakra (Gold/ Clear)

It is now scientifically well documented that we are creating our reality in every given moment (*What the Bleep Do We Know?* is a great example of this).

Enlightened Indigo individuals have an invincible belief in their own powers because they fully understand that they are spiritual beings having a human experience and therefore have the capacity to create whatever they want.

These leaders are unwavering in their dedication and discipline to allow their spirit, rather than their ego, to lead, because they understand the full power of intention, as Chiang explained to Jonathan Livingston Seagull. In business terms, they have an overwhelming magical ability to manifest for all, as does the Grameen Bank, which is a community development bank offering microcredit to the poor in Bangladesh.

They find themselves always in the right place at the right time, able to access the seemingly impossible. This is not luck: it is synchronicity.

Rumi in many ways is the energy signature for Enlightened Indigo, in particular when he writes,

Out beyond ideas of wrongdoing and rightdoing,
there is a field.
I'll meet you there.

When the soul lies down in that grass,
the world is too full to talk about.
Ideas, language, even the phrase "each other" doesn't make any sense.

Within Enlightened Indigo leaders there is fearlessness because they know that there will always be enough and that the idea of abundant spirit on the inside creates abundance on the outside. These leaders see themselves as lucky and so have a real sense of playfulness and cheekiness because they appear to have the luck of the gods; they play to that too, thereby reinforcing their image. Being around them is inspiring and they bring out the best in others. Unlike Midas, (whom we will meet later on in a parable), they are very generous with their knowledge and spread their wealth in a way that creates self-reliance.

The mantra for Enlightened Indigo is "Give and you will receive."

Blue

Figure 2.7 Throat Chakra (Blue/ Blue)

Blue stands for traditional values – upholding order with a strong belief in hierarchy and authority. It is not by chance that the colour of the UK Conservative Party is Blue, nor is it by chance that our language reflects this: we describe the police force as "the boys in blue."

<u>Positive Traits of Blue</u>

At their best, Blue leaders receive unswerving loyalty from the troops and have a commanding presence because they are natural teachers and articulate communicators that want to share and integrate their knowledge in the system. In their desire for harmony, they will eradicate conflict by building a consultative culture. They are always interested in the opinions of their staff.

Blue leaders are often found in growing organisations, as one of their strengths is their ability to bring order by designing and implementing the protocols and rules of engagement. Often these traits are associated with those in senior financial and legal positions. You will often hear them say, "What's the right thing to do here?" Due to their strong sense of duty, they are hugely reliable and won't let you down.

Blue leaders often find it easy to connect with a more left-brain orientated leadership style because they feel comfortable with facts and appreciate logical thinking. They have a tendency to favour the mind over a display of feelings because of their strong connection to the masculine. Blue leaders put their sense of duty to others ahead of consideration for themselves and their feelings.

A natural evolution for Blue leaders is to become increasingly specialised and experts in their field. This comes from their love of learning and the desire to grow their understanding and maintain a sense of progress. In business they make natural mentors. It is not uncommon to see Blue leaders emerge as thought leaders with an authoritative outlook in their field because they gain huge respect for their knowledge and analytical abilities. The mantra for Blue is "Knowledge is power".

Blue organisations pride themselves on their professionalism and often display that through the use of blue in their branding. Mintzberg's classification of organisational structures is helpful in understanding the make-up of Blue organisations. Broadly, they come in two types: either as a machine bureaucracy or a professional organisation. A police force is a good example of a machine bureaucracy, in that work is highly formalised; there are many routines and procedures, and decision-making is centralised. A large accountancy practice is a good example of a professional organisation in that it consists of knowledge workers who demand control of their own work, which leads to a large degree of specialisation and decentralised decision-making.

Negative Traits of Blue

The British trait of stoicism is most evident within the Blue leader pack and if their strength of love of tradition and duty is overplayed, they mask their emotions, seeing them as a sign of weakness in business. This leads to an inability to speak up for what they believe in for themselves and their people and they may present as aloof, cold and dictatorial. Communication can become very stilted and can breakdown as they hide behind emails, restrict the forms of online communications that they use and block face-to-face discussions.

Their lack of flexibility when it comes to change means that they can become yesterday's men and women. Preservation of the old order at all costs means they miss out on the new. The resistance that they build up inside also means that they are often very conflicted.

Another strength which can become an Achilles heel for Blue leaders is their strong sense of justice. Their desire for consistency and congruency in others' actions can become so consuming that they lose their sense of proportion.

In a cultural context, when the negative attributes of Blue are given too much sway, Blue leaders can stifle creativity and freedom of expression, as any difference of opinion is seen to be challenging to authority. The environment becomes imbalanced with "macho-style" behaviours. Whilst it always remains professional, there is an undercurrent of the "Just do what I say" mentality. For staff/employees, there is little debate or discussion in this environment, because boundaries do not feel safe.

This behaviour, if unchecked, leads to an increase in top-down communication through a flurry of memos. Other signs include obsessive control of branding messages. Conflict will be resisted at all costs because it will be viewed as a threat to order, rather than as positive breakthrough thinking.

The underlying characteristic of order is that people need to feel safe. In Blue, safety is about feeling emotionally secure and knowing where people stand so they can speak out. Unchecked, this can lead to a need for rules for everything, which is the fastest route known towards bureaucracy where all forms of innovation are curbed.

What happens in a Blue-style organisation when the strengths are overplayed can be seen by looking at the Armed Forces. An example is the deaths, between 1995 and 2002, of four young people at Deepcut, an army barracks, where initial training takes place for recruits wanting to become soldiers. Nicholas Blake QC carried out the most recent private review and he concurred with the general findings that the deaths were self-inflicted, but he also criticised a number of aspects of training at Deepcut at the time, which could have contributed to the deaths. In particular, he noted the reference to bullying – this kind of behaviour is rife in overtly Blue organisations.

Parable for Blue
The Butterfly

A man is watching a butterfly emerge from its chrysalis. He decides to help the butterfly emerge because the process appears to be taking such a long time, so he gets a pair of scissors and cuts open the cocoon. The butterfly then emerges but it has a swollen body and small, shrivelled wings and so is never able to fly as a result.

This parable epitomises some of the key lessons for Blue leaders. The man was well intentioned and his actions came out of kindness. He did not realise the value of the struggle just as Blue leaders' need for order and stillness means that they can find it hard to stand back and allow chaos in the workplace. With the butterfly, the beautiful struggle is a way of forcing fluid from the body of the butterfly into its wings so it will be ready for flight once it frees itself from the cocoon. In business, the beautiful struggle that can help shape what the organisation is becoming is often missed by Blue leaders, and if they are operating from a negative Blue perspective, they can stifle entrepreneurial activity and opportunity because it appears to flout agreed protocols.

Enlightened Blue (Blue Violet)

In this space there is a move from the mode of telling to a more subtle version of showing the way through storytelling. An archetype that personifies Enlightened Blue is the wise elder. There is respect for the ancient traditions and a knowingness about the cycle of life which means that more than anything, the opportunity to reflect is valued.

Figure 2.8 Enlightened Blue Chakra (Blue Violet/ Blue Violet)

There is a sacred element to Enlightened Blue leadership that recognises the importance of long-term decision-making. These leaders will consider the impact decisions will have on the next seven generations, because they can hold space for all the perspectives around an issue. This also enables them to embrace and model full, open, honest, and transparent communication. Everything they do is imbued with a timeless wisdom.

Enlightened Blue leaders are the wisdom keepers, invested in new ways of being and initiating others into these ideas by offering a portal to new levels of understanding. They appreciate that the voice is a powerful tool in inspiring others, unifying them and releasing resistance. Communication within Enlightened Blue starts with the intention and emerges as a bodily response linking the mind, the heart and the intuition – this is why it is so powerful. The mantra for Enlightened Blue is "Inspire through your word."

Notes

1. Dan Siegel (Random House, 2010) *Mindsight: The new science of personal transformation*

2. This is how people typically respond to change: there are the tradition keepers that resist pretty much all change because they favour the status quo (25%). There are those that sit and wait to see what happens before declaring their hand (50%); and there are the leapers (25%), who are the early adopters and revel in change. Even these early adopters have fears that can stop them from moving into their full potential.

3. Allen Sacharov (Ten Speed Press, 1988) *Offbeat Careers: The Directory of Unusual Work*

4. Robert Greenleaf's philosophy of servant leadership had its roots from reading a work of fiction in 1958: "The idea of the servant as leader came out of reading Hermann Hesse's *Journey to the East*. In this story, we see a band of men on a mythical journey... The central figure of the story is Leo, who accompanies the party as the servant who does their menial chores, but who also sustains them with his spirit and his song. He is a person of extraordinary presence. All goes well until Leo disappears. Then the group falls into disarray and the journey is abandoned. They cannot make it without the servant Leo. The narrator, one of the party, after some years of wandering, finds Leo and is taken into the Order that had sponsored the journey. There he discovers that Leo, whom he had known first as servant, was in fact the titular head of the Order, its guiding spirit, a great and noble leader. Greenleaf's essay "Servant as Leader" inspires people all over the world.

5. If you want to understand this in greater detail, see Hawkins' map of consciousness which calibrates different qualities from shame to enlightenment with courage seen as the midpoint, on a scale from 20–1,000.

6. Source is used throughout this book to mean God, whatever is bigger than humans and gives life more meaning.

CHAPTER 4:

Green

This is the mid-point on our journey through the seven fundamental colours; as such, Green gets a whole chapter to itself. This is because it acts as the gateway between the first three colours (Violet, Indigo and Blue) and the last three (Yellow, Orange and Red). Green is made from combining a cool colour (Blue) and a warm colour (Yellow) – it is the opening which pulls in all the colours.

Green is the colour of the heart chakra and is therefore love; and in *The KK Systems™*, it interacts with all the colours in fascinating ways. You cannot have meaningful communication (Blue) without empathy – a core component of love; you will find it hard to access your intuition (Indigo) as a leader if you are ego-driven, and that means you have forgotten about love; and it will be impossible to embody trust (Violet) without deep self-compassion, which is also a component of love. Transformation only comes when your confidence (Yellow) is based on a strong sense of self-worth, which happens when you can embrace all of who you are with love. You can only build connected relationships with others (Orange) when you have a loving relationship with yourself; you will start thriving by manifesting what you need (Red) when you recognise you are never alone because love has shown you the interconnections. The other six foundational colours form a cohesion which leads to more congruency between thoughts, feelings and actions – if you manage to integrate them through the Green of the heart chakra.

Green

The characteristics that underpin Green in our terminology can be referenced by *The Great Turning*, Joanna Macy's work on how to affect wholesale change. She has identified three elements: actions to slow the damage to the Earth and those that inhabit it; an analysis of structural causes and the creation of alternatives; and shifting consciousness. Her work calls for a systemic way of thinking and being.

Figure 3.0 Heart Chakra (Green/ Green)

The more we understand the natural world that we inhabit and the fact that every action we take has an impact on it, the greater our appreciation of it will grow. An example that illustrates that is sharks. Sharks have two serious counts against them. For many years they have been personified as predators of humans (cf. the movie *Jaws*), and in some Eastern countries, shark fin soup is highly desirable. Given this combination, it has been deemed okay to hunt them almost to extinction. As scientists are now showing us through their research, we have much to learn from these creatures. For example, a greater understanding of the nature of sharkskin has led to the development of high-tech swim suits for Olympic level swimmers. Developers claim the suits, based on the hydrodynamics of a shark's skin, shave off fractions of a second on the swimmer's overall time.

Our increasingly digitally connected world shows us first-hand the impact of population explosion, deforestation, climate disruption, polluted ecosystems and the worrying whole scale extinction of plant and animal species. As we begin to recognise the preciousness of the world we live in, we seek to preserve more of it. This is only possible if we open our hearts to the beauty of the world around us and then choose to both pursue different goals from those that epitomise our current economy, and seek alternative pleasures. This means evolving new values and giving monetary value to areas that are currently considered valueless.

A concrete example of this is the cost of mobile phones. For some time the New Economics Foundation, among others, has called for the proper pricing of goods as a way to stop the wholesale destruction of our world. For example, if mobile phones were priced to include the actual cost of extracting precious minerals out of the habitat of silver-backed gorillas, consumers would think twice about upgrading their mobile phones.

So what does this signify for business? On so many levels, the growing awareness impacts us as consumers and creates more ecological products and services. Biomimicry is a brilliant example of this. If we take a closer look at birds in nature, they boost the distance which they can fly by 70% through the use of the V shape. Scientists have discovered that when a flock takes on the familiar V formation, as one bird flaps its wings, it creates a small updraft, which lifts the bird behind. As each bird passes, they add their own energy to the stroke, helping all the birds maintain flight. By rotating their order through the stack they spread out their exertion. A group of researchers at Stanford University thinks that passenger airlines could realise fuel savings by using the same tactic. By travelling in a V shape with planes taking turns in front like birds do, aircraft could use 15% less fuel compared to flying solo.

<u>Positive Characteristics of Green</u>

As we start to understand how we connect to the whole in terms of our natural environment and its inhabitants, it is natural for us to spend time reflecting and want to transform our level of thinking to bring greater balance and, in so doing, appreciate full diversity. This gives us the inspiration to activate heart-based values because we have stopped tinkering on the outside and have started to delve into the depths of our core. It is from this place that we see it all comes back to us, each of us; therefore, when we are working from our integrity and what we love is based on sound values, we give and receive more. It creates a circle of appreciation.

What do Green leaders look like? Green leaders have clarity regarding their guiding values and responsibilities, both individually and collectively. They have an appreciation that the environment impacts on everything and therefore, they have a congruence of actions and values. The prevailing Green culture is based on the analogy that the sum of the parts is greater than the individual. Green companies create employee and consumer trust; they give a lot of freedom to their employees because they understand that rest and renewal and space for clarity and reflection are all pre-requisites to breakthrough thinking. You will often find senior HR managers with strong Green tendencies.

Mark Silver, who founded Heart of Business in 2001, epitomises the qualities of a Green leader. Using Sufi-based practices, he has developed a heart-based wisdom curriculum that focuses on helping business owners develop their brand by coming from their heart whilst incorporating nitty-gritty business practices. He has had a great deal of success and has expanded from being a solopreneur coach to hiring a team of people to work with him.

An image that demonstrates a facet of this colour is that of green shoots, which are representative of a learning and growth orientation. Companies who sit specifically in this spectrum invest heavily in learning and development. There is a dynamic pace and energy in Green organisations because of the clear focus on health and wellbeing – from the canteen to the gym; and there is an understanding that inspiration received from the natural environment is as inspirational as that received from the written word.

As an obvious example of a Green organisation, we cite the company Aveda, which was formally acquired by the Estee Lauder companies in 1997. Aveda is the embodiment of the ideas of Horst Rechelbacher, who was a pioneer in plant-based personal care and aromatherapy and an active environmentalist who changed the world of beauty. Aveda's mission is to set an example for environmental leadership and responsibility – not just in the world of beauty, but in all areas of business. A-Veda means "all-knowledge" in Sanskrit. Its roots are planted in Ayurveda, the ancient healing art of India, and also in other indigenous wisdoms that take a holistic approach to life and wellness, and which focus on cultivating balance. The company ensures integrity and quality by using organically grown flowers and plants wherever possible and by building relationships with indigenous people, farmers and brokers who are in alignment with its philosophy of sustainable agriculture. Their whole focus in everything they do is based on their "reduce, reuse, recycle" ethos.

Specific examples of initiatives that Aveda has spearheaded include:

1. An ongoing partnership with the Yawanawa Tribe of the Brazilian Amazon
    This partnership has helped to sustain the Yawanawa Tribe while bringing attention to the plight of their disappearing rainforest home.

2. Partnering with a community collective
    In 1995, Aveda partnered with the babassu nut breakers of the Brazilia Amazon, who had formed to obtain certified organic babassu for use in the creation of a foaming cleansing element known as "babassu betaine". Aveda has financed the construction of, and training for, a babassu-processing facility, a soap-making facility and a paper press for processing babassu fibres. Aveda does not test their products on animals rather on willing human participants.

3. Setting a precedent in the haircare industry
    Aveda introduced an aerosol hairspray that has a net-zero impact on the Earth's climate, and an award-winning low, 35% VOC formula.

4. Funding wind turbines through a partnership with NativeEnergy, an organisation that supports and builds renewable energy products, Aveda has helped fund wind turbines. Aveda claims that it purchases enough wind energy to power its primary manufacturing facility.

Negative Traits of Green

Green leaders are naturally caring, co-operative and team-focused which makes them exceptionally approachable and considerate; however, they may succumb to the subtle manipulation tactics of others and can be slow to let go of employees that no longer serve the organisation.

In an extreme form of this, Green leaders can have favourites and promote certain behaviours over others; this can lead to the unconscious formation of cliques. If unstopped, jealousy and envy become rife within the organisation and HR issues zap the energy and attention of those at the top. This can lead to a lack of boundary management, which in turn leads to overwhelm and people pleasing behaviour in middle management and frontline staff. Deference then becomes the order of the day along with a large dose of brown-nosing.

A parable that helps unpack Green further is the Wizard of Oz. This is not because the Emerald City is green. Rather it is because it is a metaphor for giving yourself space to see who you truly are. Dorothy only realised her own power after she was taken out of her natural environment by a cyclone which carried her to a magical land.

Parable for Green
The Wizard of Oz

Dorothy represents that naive youthful innocence that can get taken in by politicians/ salesmen in business. She is trying to find her way home through searching on the outside. She arrives in the Emerald City, a spectacle of opulence and wealth and yet when she looks behind the curtain, there is no substance – it is all smoke and mirrors, conducted by a wily, manipulative wizard. Her companions demonstrate the timeless qualities of courage and standing up for what you believe in. At the crux of it all, heart-based intelligence as represented by the Lion means more than intellectual knowledge. The Scarecrow represents the natural world, the Tin Man represents the mechanical one, the Emerald City represents the value of money and the yellow brick road is the path to enlightenment. At the end of the story, when she recognises that the Wizard is as vulnerable as she is and he doesn't have the answer, Dorothy realises she herself possesses the keys to her own destiny and does not need anything or anyone to bring about the transformation she desires. She begins to appreciate herself and her own resourcefulness.

Have you, as a leader, ever doubted your own abilities and in doing so brought about circumstances that have borne out the doubt? The wisdom here is to appreciate that connection to self is vital and it is the starting point to unfolding the magic.

Enlightened Green (Lilac/ Pink)

Figure 3.1 Enlightened Green Chakra (Lilac/ Pink)

The qualities of Enlightened Green are quite far removed from our business reality of today, and difficult to encapsulate in words without appearing trite, so we decided to paint a picture using an example of someone who personified this vibration: Nelson Mandela. Mandela was admired by millions, and tackled a seemingly impossible situation in that he was required to unite a disparate people who had been separated by race for more than a generation. It took great wisdom and compassion to let go of old injustices and not seek retribution. His action led to increased stability and ultimately the opportunity of prosperity for all. It took grace to ask only for truth and reconciliation in a country which had experienced untold suffering and separation for over 30 years. It was only possible because Mandela believed in enlightened service.

Not surprisingly, Enlightened Green shows us spiritual intelligence in its most pure form – wonderful outcomes can be created from impossible odds, due to faith, trust and the inner knowing that good

113

can, and will, prevail. This is only possible when we can see the potential good in people, however they show up. Never has this been so important as now with the bombings in Europe and the Middle East. The current subsequent reactions meet violence with more atrocities. More fighting will beget more fighting.

The key to Enlightened Green is self-transcendence. This is what we saw in the recently televised film *Song for Jenny,* the true story of Jennifer Nicholls who died in the 7/7 bombings in London. The film shows the unfolding of the day and the impact of Jenny's death on her family. The person who struggles the most to come to terms with her death is her mother. It seems senseless to her – this cutting down of a 24-year-old girl in her prime who had never hated anyone. She is desperate to make sense of it and insists on seeing photographs of her dead daughter, on visiting her body so she can say goodbye; and going to the scene of the bombing. It also puts an enormous strain on her marriage, as she is unable to share how she feels with anyone in her family and thinks that, as she is a priest, she must be strong for them all. And yet this tested her faith to the limits because she lost the person most precious to her for no justifiable reason. She could have turned away from her faith; instead her daughter's death helped her restore her sense of faith in humanity as a whole as she was able to forgive the perpetrators by holding compassion in her heart for them. This is the kind of act that embodies self-transcendence.

CHAPTER 5:

Yellow, Orange and Red

This chapter focuses on the last three of the seven fundamental colours. Yellow, which is all about mental clarity, focuses on the role of expertise in leadership; Orange holds exuberance and creativity, and is at the core of outstanding relationships. And these relationships only flourish if built on solid foundations, in Red. These are also the three core, base chakras which, if they are not balanced, will derail any leader.

Yellow

Figure 4.0 Solar Plexus Chakra (Yellow/ Yellow)

With its underlying belief that everything is pre-determined, Newtonian Physics shaped the current construct or paradigm in which we live today. Determinists believe that everything that happens can be defined through cause and effect. This means that the concept of free will is a myth. The illusion of choice is simply a coping and survival mechanism that allows us to function in the world. Determinists tend to take a reductionist perspective on everything.

In a personal context, this means that people are broken and need fixing. In a business context, all tasks are broken down into their smallest component parts. Everything is considered to be separate. In linear thought, the past creates the present and the present creates the future. When you have solved a problem, it goes away.

This is all relevant when considering the characteristics of Yellow, where the emphasis is on logic and reason. Historically, this emphasis evolved from Newton's discoveries, which led to a need to provide an evidence base for any theory or new idea. Without that, a discovery has little validity in a world which worships research and empirical thinking. The essence of Yellow in the spectrum is about meeting one's mental needs through exercising intellectual enquiry and being focused.

Typically, Yellow leaders will use phrases like *Where are the facts? Prove it to me!* They can become quite impatient if things seem to be taking too long and are known to interject discussions with *What's your point?* or *Get to the point!*

Chris Anderson, the man who made TED what it is today, is a great example of a Yellow leader because he is full of ideas: he became a deep knowledge expert in new media before being approached by Wurman to be his successor at TED. In 2001 Anderson's Sapling Foundation, whose motto is *Fostering the spread of great ideas,* acquired TED. TED Talks really started to gain in popularity after April 2007 when the new website was published and all talks became freely available to watch and download over the Internet.

Yellow organisations place a premium on knowledge – more so than anyone else within the knowledge economy. Think about the Big Four – the four largest professional services networks, offering audit, assurance, tax consulting, advisory, actuarial, corporate finance and legal services – with their focus on knowledge management systems and databases. They actively want to be seen as experts in their field because it is a differentiating factor that allows them to dictate their price to the market.

They are able to use their expertise in the information and knowledge space to collect, provide and design tools that measure, for example, the impact of social capital. It is all about codifying data, knowing the bottom line, having the structures and processes in place and being defined by orderly frameworks and models.

Yellow organisations are full of responsible folk who feel duty-bound and want to compete to be the best.

PwC is a classic example of a Yellow organisation. Its ethos harks back to Taylorism[1] as in: if you cannot measure it or quantify it, then it is not important. The reputation of the organisation is based on its ability to analyse and synthesise data. This is probably in part because of its roots in accountancy. In 2010 there was a major rebrand and the name ceased to be PricewaterhouseCoopers and became "pwc", all in lower case to encourage a sense of informality; it gave more emphasis to its consultancy business by using a palette of warm colours like pink, red, yellow and orange in its logo rather than the grey and blue of old. This was largely a cosmetic move however, as the underlying principles did not change.

Positive Attributes of Yellow

Yellow leaders are always looking for achievement and wanting to take charge; they are progressive and action oriented. Their focus is on the intellectualisation of processes at the expense of feeling because the best results are achieved only by refining the process. This only happens if you are methodical and use a step-by-step approach.

Qualities associated with Yellow leaders are joy and optimism. This joy is more about an enthusiasm that emerges from the discovery of new ideas. It is an intellectual curiosity for what is presenting from a head perspective rather than an embodied feeling. The mantra for Yellow is "Logic rules".

Negative Attributes of Yellow

Getting lost in the pursuit of knowledge can lead to overthinking everything and becoming submerged in the detail of the data. In their need for clarity and precision, Yellow leaders will often lose sight of the bigger picture.

And when they spend too much time in complexity thinking, their energy becomes blocked. This manifests itself in the form of analysis paralysis, indecision, and high stress levels, which in turn start to impact adversely on teams in the form of negative behaviours and criticism. At this point, Yellow leaders can be a tad paranoid and overly sceptical, which can present as controlling behaviours. This instils fear amongst staff and neurotic "A" type behaviour in both employees and the Yellow leaders themselves, with their tendency towards overachieving to banish the thought that they are only as good as their last project.

When this happens, Yellow leaders tend to believe that they know best and so they dig their heels in, refusing to see that there may be other perspectives in the situation. This rigidity in thinking will often lead to a stalemate when they come up against other Yellow leaders, as neither side is willing to concede on a matter of principle. It can lead to power struggles within an organisation and there is often a feeling of a lack of consultation. The negative Yellow leaders' mantra is "Let's just get on with it".

Their insecurity shows up in the way that they project their lack of self-worth onto others. For them, there is no time to feel into what is the right thing to do; the emphasis is on doing. This creates an organisation full of tension.

Parable for Yellow
The Hare and the Tortoise

Another way of deepening the understanding of Yellow is through the parable of The Hare and the Tortoise. The parable is not written out in full here because so many know the story – an assumption we are happy to make.

The honing of the intellect was the principal focal point for Yellow leaders in their early life and because of this, there is a danger that they will fall into a form of intellectual snobbery around their own ability and its limitations. This blindness to their weaknesses means they have a tendency to brag about their capabilities and be rather over confident about what they can achieve, which makes some of them great candidates for being the hare in this story.

At their best, Yellow leaders are thorough and methodical. They take their time to assess the different elements of any given situation before reaching a decision, trusting in their innate knowledge of the subject. Because they are experts, they have the ability to recognise patterns almost at a subliminal level. In this sense, some Yellow leaders are more aligned with the tortoise.

Enlightened Yellow (Gold/ Gold)

Figure 4.1 Enlightened Yellow Chakra (Gold/ Gold)

Because it does not include reductionist principles, Gold offers us a generative outlook on leaders and their organisations. In Gold there is only the now and infinite possibilities. No one needs fixing and a culture of curiosity prevails. There is an understanding that we live in a subjective world, that there is no objective truth, and that everything is connected and order comes out of chaos.

This is the world of breakthroughs, of quantum leaps, new possibilities, endless renewals. In this space, leaders stand in their power and are happy to have the visibility that goes with that. This is because they have done their inner work and in turn have also been shaped by the outer twists of fate. They epitomise wisdom that can only come from self-discovery and it is this that enables them to fully embrace an authentic way of being.

As they have discovered their own Gold, they recognise that self-promotion is not the endgame and they focus instead on the quality of the work that they are delivering. Their mantra is "Be careful what you wish for". They don't push because they have that secure innate knowingness around their own attractiveness.

It is difficult to cite examples of this in the traditional corporate space because these leaders get on with the work without creating a fuss or a stir. An archetypal Gold is represented by the pioneer who can always see the opportunity in the presenting issue and can change course based on an awareness that is honed via an instinctive tuning into the upcoming trends, rather than relying on a base of knowledge.

The character types that sit firmly in Gold consciousness tend to be self-employed because it is the ultimate expression of self and freedom and requires great resilience. We can think of no better example than the out-there, trailblazing, trendsetting Seth Godin, who has also become known as the preeminent entrepreneur for the Information Age. He is an American writer who's published 17 books addressing various aspects of marketing, advertising, business ventures and leadership. He rose to fame for public speaking when he uploaded his ebook *Unleashing the Ideavirus.* He made it available to the general public for free. His first start-up, Yoyodyne, was one of the first Internet-based direct marketing firms whose revolutionary ideas on how companies should reach their target audiences attracted companies like Volvo, Microsoft and Sony Music. He then went on to found Squidoo.com, a website where users can share links or information about an idea or topic of their choice. His aim is to make information available to everyone in a world in which everyone from anywhere can play an active role. In 2003 he wrote *Purple Cow*, which focuses on how to transform your business by being remarkable.

Gold principles include the ability to go beyond preaching and into teaching practical ways using storytelling as a way to capture the imagination and show others how to be their own leader. Godin shares all about how to create your own social following in *Tribes*, because he recognises both his own power and that he is unique and therefore no one can copy him. Even if you mimic what he has done, it will never be the same. This gives him a fearlessness to reveal all, rather than drip-feeding a few pieces of information over a time. Gold leaders, like Godin, are game changers because they are changing industries through the way they see the world.

Godin is changing the book publishing industry. In his latest offering, *What To Do When It's Your Turn,* he offers us an alternative book almost in the form of a magazine with the opportunity to buy multiple copies at a discounted price for sharing. He is tapping into the spirit of connection and a rising desire of people everywhere to create the change they want to see in the world. He recognises that it is about creating leaders and replacements, not followers. Gold people see the world as multifaceted, which enables them to create links which others do not see and to make lateral leaps that can revolutionise the world. It takes clarity of vision and resilience. Gold leaders in organisations hire those that are better than they because they have moved beyond ego, are plugged in and connected.

Orange

Figure 4.2 Sacral Chakra (Orange/ Orange)

Creativity is a core component of Orange. Deepak Chopra said in 2015 that *All creativity is a break in logic*, in recognition of the vital part that it plays in developing the new leadership consciousness. Neuroscience now shows us that creativity, a natural aspect of each and every one of us, flourishes where individuals experience consistently positive emotional states and have enough space for reflection and review; these in turn stimulate curiosity.

So how can we access our full creative force? An easy springboard to full creative self-expression is through the sense of play as that puts us in touch with our inner child. As transformational coaches, we recognise that each person is naturally creative, resourceful and whole. Many people fail to recognise this because of the deep conditioning they experienced as children either from their parents or through the education they received.[2] In childhood, we learnt self-defence strategies to manage difficult and uncomfortable situations and feelings, and as adults, these can trip us up and we don't even realise it because most of those strategies have become unconscious patterns of behaviour. The wounded child, often triggered by challenging confrontations and situations, can present at any time. At any age, we can still learn the essence of play: it is the route to full creative expression.

Orange embraces all aspects of the emotional. It's all about how we feel and how we share that with the world both consciously and unconsciously. NLP has helped us to realise that 90% of all learning is unconscious. The key 19 attributes of the unconscious mind are as follows:

1. It stores all your memories
2. It organises all your memories by timeline and subject (Gestalt)
3. It's the domain of your emotions
4. It represses memories with unresolved negative emotions
5. It presents repressed emotions for resolution though may keep the repressed memory from your conscious mind to protect you
6. It runs your body – it has a blueprint for your body as it is now and as it is in perfect health
7. It preserves your body
8. It follows the moral code you were taught and accepted
9. It wants to serve and follow instructions from your conscious mind
10. It is responsible for storing, distributing and transmitting the energy in your body
11. It receives all information from your senses and filters it and passes the remaining perceptions to the conscious mind
12. It maintains all your instincts and generates habits
13. It requires repetition for a new habit to be installed
14. It is programmed to continually seek more and more
15. It uses and responds to symbols

16. It takes everything personally
17. It always follows the path of least effort
18. It doesn't process negatives
19. It works best as a whole, integrated unit: when the conscious and unconscious mind are aligned

When we feel good about our learning experience, it is easy for us to take things in and be fully aware of the impact we are having and therefore have greater access to our full range of creativity.

Typically overt Orange leaders are generally optimistic, larger-than-life personalities and very gregarious; they often mask deep wounds. They are self-starters, hugely resourceful, creative and full of ideas. They have high emotional intelligence and can sense the underlying patterns in their world. A mature expression of a fully actualised Orange leader is one who recognises their own needs and the needs of others and therefore has a reputation for collaborative ways of working.

An Orange culture is one where banter predominates and it can be refreshing and uplifting. That good dose of humour means there is a tendency to not take oneself too seriously. There is a solid sense of being part of a team, and supporting that ethos is key in an Orange environment.

A good example of a well-known Orange leader is Richard Branson. Like Marmite, people love him or hate him. At his essence, he is hugely creative and prepared to take risks, so there is a quasi-dangerous, edgy quality to him. His success has come from his focus on building relationships, making that the heart of the Virgin Brand, and doing whatever it takes to put people at their ease.

If you look at the Virgin portfolio, at first glance there would appear to be no logic to the makeup of companies within it because the links are so subtle. But at the core is innovation and making improvements.

Positive Aspects of Orange

Orange leaders have a charismatic, magnetic attraction, which could be called sex appeal. This is because they are strongly connected to their feeling sense and as such, find it easy to build relationships. They know how to make people feel special and unique – it is easy to be mesmerised by them. Their leadership style is fully inclusive and emotionally intelligent. There's that sense of fun and banter plus a richness of cultural diversity and respect for difference. Orange leaders can bring out the best in others because they know themselves and sense inadequacies in others. The mantra for Orange is "Relationships count".

The classical archetypal Orange leader often has to overcome emotional challenges in early childhood which can set them apart from the group. One of these challenges is dyslexia, which is characteristic of a number of Orange leaders in both the positive and the negative. As more is discovered about dyslexia, it is clear that it brings many gifts to compensate for the challenges people get with it.

Dyslexia brings gifts as well as challenges. It is now known that dyslexics' brains are wired differently. According to the research, their visual and spatial skills are often at a superior level, but they struggle in areas like reading, writing and spelling. They are focused in this way because a key component of Orange is the ability to see things differently; it tends to be a powerhouse of innovation.

Lord Sugar, Anita Roddick, Richard Branson, Jamie Oliver and IKEA founder Ingvar Kamprad overcame their dyslexia to create hugely successful businesses, and research suggests dyslexics are disproportionately represented among entrepreneurs. Julie Logan, emeritus professor of entrepreneurship at Cass Business School in London, says that 20% of the UK's business self-starters have the condition. Her research into the US market showed that 35% of company founders identified themselves as dyslexic, compared with 15% in the general population. She then compared the traits, attributes and early experiences of people who identified as dyslexic from a sample of entrepreneurs who were not dyslexic.

Dyslexic entrepreneurs reported as good or excellent at oral communication, delegation, creative and spatial awareness tasks, whilst non-dyslexics reported as average or good, Logan says. People with dyslexia, she found, tend to compensate for things they can't do well by developing excellence in other areas: oral communication, delegation (because they must learn to trust other people with tasks they can't do from an early age), as well as problem-solving and people management.

Negative Aspects of Orange

Operating in the negative, an Orange culture breeds far too much dependency and neediness because of its underlying saboteur qualities, which cause employees to feel that they are not good enough. Deep down, Orange leaders have a strong need for external validation and acceptance and want to be needed. They have such enthusiasm for looking good that they cannot say no to any high status project; this means that they often set up unrealistic expectations which conceal simmering "martyr-like" behaviour.

As they cannot see their own pattern, they set themselves up for failure time and time again until they finally begin to appreciate that present-day circumstances and work conflicts are often caused by an overly-strong sense of identity and ego. Challenges on the path come along where there is a preoccupation with needing to fit in with the current cultural framework of a business. Being natural relationship builders, Orange leaders are instinctive collaborators – they have the social skills to get ideas started and off the ground; yet if they are not clear and don't speak up enough about what they are feeling, they repress their feelings until they can no longer contain them and so explode in an emotional outburst.

They love change and are always looking for the next big idea. This is fine in itself, but if this strength is overplayed, it can lead to "Toad of Toad Hall behaviour": the desire to adopt the latest fad before the current one has been fully implemented and experienced. Finishing projects is not a quality that is valued in overtly Orange organisations. Orange leaders can be seduced quite easily by those that talk a good talk and when this happens, they become unstuck. This is further emphasised by their extrovert tendencies, which lead to going from one high to the next without pausing for breath. Unstopped, this can end up in burnout or a shallowness due to a lack of introspection.

For Orange leaders, the focus is on building a strong internal network at the expense of contacts outside of the organisation.

Success comes from the level of influence within the system. If there is an over-emphasis on this, then many of the positive features of Orange such as the ability to communicate and connect instantaneously with others implode. Information that was shared in confidence can be used against another and life becomes very personal, as wounded leaders use that data to destabilise their people and shut them down. What we see at play here is the use of subtle tactics to undermine others. At its extreme this can show up as a form of indirect violence and bullying – an outward projection of the inner insecurity.

Parable for Orange
The Three Little Pigs

The parable that illustrates the characteristics of Orange is *The Three Little Pigs*, wherein the main message is the importance of self-development, self-acceptance and resilience. The only house able to repel the attacks by the wolf was the one made of bricks: the two made of straw and sticks were too flimsy.

Each house is a metaphor of the foundations on which we construct our sense of self. If, like the first two pigs, we don't take the time to consider our purpose through introspection from time to time and brick by brick, then we can be easily swayed because we don't have a strong sense of what matters and who we are. And the third little pig's act of generosity to invite the other two to share his home even though their laziness had led to a fatal shortcut is a perfect illustration of how we can go beyond judgement, offer each other support in times of need and collaborate effectively.

Enlightened Orange (Orange/ Rose Pink)

Figure 4.3 Enlightened Orange (Orange/ Rose Pink)

In Enlightened Orange, there is a move towards interdependence: everyone models the honest expression of feelings. There is a demonstrable focus on appreciation and recognising each other's worth and talents rather than focusing on what's missing. There is already a wealth of material in the mainstream aimed at pinpointing innate talent as opposed to learnt skill; see for example Zenger Folkman's talent profiling and Gallop's Strength Finder approach. This shift has occurred due to increased awareness of Positive Psychology, founded by Martin Seligman.[3] It is the scientific study of the strengths that enable individuals and communities to thrive. The field is founded on the belief that people want to lead meaningful and fulfilling lives, to cultivate what is best within themselves, and to enhance their experiences of love, work, and play: Enlightened Orange at its best.

Contrary to today's market place where there is much focus on the lack of trust in organisations, in the world of Enlightened Orange there is no requirement for formalised meetings nor the need for office presenteeism, as the underlying trust of others and self-ownership is evident. Furthermore there is also recognition of the need to personalise and tailor motivational messages as a way of underlining the value of individuality and difference. This leads to an increased sense of inspiration.

One person who embodied many of the qualities of Enlightened Orange, Dame Anita Roddick, set up her first Body Shop in Brighton in 1976. At that time, lotions and potions were laboratory tested, industrially concocted and sold through the many chemist chains and salons more interested in image than content. Roddick caught the mood of the moment and understood how women wanted to nurture and present themselves.

There was an honest communication about what the products could do for women rather than the usual hype that focused on wrinkle reduction. There was sensuous fun to her marketing too that appealed to a more conscious audience. She conveyed that not only was it okay to have fun at work but that it could lead to worthy outcomes – she did not distinguish between business and her passion for considering environmental and ethical issues.

Like so many who convey the positive Orange attributes, Roddick had her fair share of shock and trauma, starting with the discovery that her father's cousin, who would later become her stepfather, was actually her real dad. In later life, she contracted hepatitis C which led to cirrhosis of the liver; she died of a brain haemorrhage at the age of 64.

Money did not change Roddick; she remained true to her values throughout her lifetime. What made her an Enlightened Orange leader was her complete non-conformity whilst maintaining a total appreciation for the interdependence of the world. For example, she started the no-packaging and refill options years before recycling and concern about the environment became commonplace. She understood that, if there was love and attention given by the people making the Brazil nut conditioner over in Brazil, it would have a multiplier effect wherever it was sold.

Roddick was also at the forefront of recognising the power of the consumer to affect change. In 1988 she wrote the foreword for the Green Consumer Guide. On the one hand, she inspired legions of people through her actions, and by actively listening to others, thereby recognising the whole person; and on the other, she had little time for those she considered to be representatives of the old paradigm, referring to them as "dinosaurs in pinstripes".

Close associates have described her as having equal measures of self-belief and vulnerability. Creating an intrapreneurial culture and being innovative were second nature to her. She epitomised a style of communication that was centred round heart-based values decades before that became an in-vogue expression, and made decisions based on intuitive insight. The mantra for Enlightened Orange is "Connect to self first and then others".

Red

Figure 4.4 Root chakra (Red/ Red)

We will use Maslow's hierarchy of human needs as a reference point here for understanding what Red is really about, in so much as it is impossible to consider serving others if you are still unable to feed, clothe and support yourself.

Red is all about our material needs, personal safety and security. It embodies the physical more than any other colour; its position in the body (at the root/ base) certainly supports this, as it sits closest to the earth.

In business terms, Red is all about the money and ensuring a positive cash flow and the attributes that relate to this. This means having effective systems in place to collect, manage and report the financials.

Red leaders can be quite flash; they can also be very directive, with a tendency to tell people what to do and to spell it out rather than allowing people to show their initiative and perhaps fill in the gaps. They are generally charismatic and competent, verging on brash, with an outward display of confidence which can often mask an insecure core. As builders, they tend to create a culture of "fit in or fuck off" because, since they believe that they know best, there is no need to consult anyone else.

They tend to hire in their own mould. The culture is typically quite insular and often rejects difference. Their mantra is "It's my way or the highway", and they like clarity in all things; consequently, from a work perspective, they will simplify everything down to its component parts. They are strong advocates of Taylorism and are very much creatures of the mechanical paradigm.

Red leaders have to keep on keeping on because work is all about survival of the fittest; they live in an ever-increasing competitive (Porter's five forces[4]) environment where people are dispensable assets and business typically ends up commoditised. Price becomes the determining factor and often the greatest influence is held by the CFO.

Positive Attributes of Red

Red leaders are achievement and results driven materialists who are passionate about what they know and what they bring to the table. At their very best they will have a sense of urgency and a clear sense of order in terms of priorities, with a finger on the pulse. Never content with business as usual, they always want more profit, more productivity and more efficiency. They are very good at focusing on whatever is the key task at any given point and so can be relied on to deliver every time. They are dynamic go-getters who love the sense of responsibility and being in charge and they keep communication simple.

Reds thrive in environments where the emphasis is cut and thrust, with an almost obsessional focus on ROI and quarterly reporting. They have an appetite for action. They make decisions quickly, having marshalled all the relevant facts.

The least comfortable with ambiguity of all leaders within the colour spectrum, Red leaders typically seek or create transparency around the rules of engagement. They are practical, grounded and solutions-focused. Employees always know where they stand with them and what they expect from them.

A man who personifies this is Jack Cohen, the Tesco PLC founder of pile it high sell it cheap fame. He built a successful brand, using many of the Red principles – a keen eye for price, sound processes, supply chain efficiencies and global expansion. The brand colours are, interestingly, blue and red.

Negative Aspects of Red

Red leaders tend to have a very short fuse and limited amounts of patience. This, coupled with their need for directness, can alienate them from the workforce, creating an us-and-them culture which leads to blame, victimhood and sacrifice. In addition, because conforming to the norm results in rewards, Reds tend to sacrifice everything, including their family, to the needs of the company. There is very little room for individuality or space to have a life.

In their desire for control, negative Red leaders inadvertently set up a parent-child mentality in the workplace; this breeds paranoia and fear because people dare not contradict them publicly and they therefore behave subversively. Gossip is rife, along with a blame mentality, which only serve to separate those who command and those who follow the orders. A corresponding outcome of this is increasing absenteeism and high staff turnover, often accentuated by slash-and-burn tactics. This is further exacerbated by the tendency to over-emphasise the value of extrinsic versus intrinsic motivation.

These extreme measures are suitable in a turnaround situation, but are unsustainable when it is business as (un)usual; they manifest the eat-or-be-eaten culture. Crisis management is the flavour of the day, which just leads to more chaos. If this is maintained, a takeover, already mooted, becomes more of an imminent reality.

The root represents systems, and in this stagnant workplace full of anger and frustration, morale is low and systems become blocked. Often presenteeism is the knee-jerk response to counter failing productivity. This is a direct reflection of the act-first-think-later modus operandi that prevails in a Red culture that is full of worker bees.

An extreme example of a negative Red leader can be seen in the fictional character Gordon Gekko in *Wall Street* (1987) and its follow-up *Money Never Sleeps* (2010). He was famed for saying *Greed is Good.*

And if we look at Tesco at the beginning of 2016, it looked as if everything had unravelled. There were serious investigations by the fraud squad, and yet in the last quarter of 2016 it appears to be on the way back up.[5]

Parable for Red
Goldilocks and the Three Bears

Goldilocks and the Three Bears is the perfect parable for Red. It is no coincidence that Goldilocks had blonde hair, as in many cultures it is a stereotypical sign of attractiveness. This appeals to base instinct which is centred round procreation. Setting the story in the house of the three bears and having Goldilocks sample each bear's porridge, chair and bed before choosing Baby Bear's food, seat and bed gives an emphasis on safety and shelter. When Goldilocks is discovered, she runs out of the cottage never to return again. This demonstrates subtly that greed cannot be satiated through acquiring more. At an unconscious level there is another layer of meaning. Replete after eating Baby Bear's porridge, Goldilocks falls asleep in his bed. Similarly in Red, when we become too complacent about our success, we become oblivious to the bad habits and behaviours which can unravel us.

Enlightened Red (Clear/ Clear)

Figure 4.5 Enlightened Red (Clear/ Clear)

The trend has been moving away from overt Red tendencies, which focus on getting more at the expense of everything else, towards the formation of more socially conscious business. In Enlightened Red, we move away from Red competitive companies to those that recognise that everything is interconnected. And there are those caught in the middle, torn by the same measures as Red companies, i.e. they recognise the role of profit growth, but they are canny enough to realise that they won't appeal to Millennials and other customers unless they appear to emulate some of their values. Often we see these companies making token gestures in this direction with correspondingly incongruent behaviour such as making a nod towards corporate social responsibility – not because they are fully behind it but to fit in with societal expectations. The mantra for Enlightened Red is "There's something for everyone."

An example of an Enlightened Red leader is John Mackey, co-founder and co-CEO of Whole Foods Market, which has become a $14 billion Fortune 500 company with more than 410 stores and 88,000 team members in three countries. The company has been included on *Fortune* magazine's "100 Best Companies to Work For" list for 18 consecutive years. A strong believer in free market principles,

133

Mackey also co-founded the Conscious Capitalism Movement (http://consciouscapitalism.org/) and co-authored a *New York Times* and *Wall Street Journal* bestselling book entitled *Conscious Capitalism: Liberating the Heroic Spirit of Business* (Harvard Business Review Press, 2013) to boldly defend and re-imagine capitalism, and encourage a way of doing business that is grounded in ethical consciousness. Mackey cut his pay to $1 in 2006 and continues to work for Whole Foods Market out of passion to see the business realise its potential for deeper purpose, and for the joy of leading a great company.

Today, in many regards, we are not experiencing the same degree of depth of revolutionary change that we witnessed in the industrial era. However, even those companies that appear to be in this no man's land of neither one nor the other are playing their part in shifting leadership consciousness into more enlightened territory by making what was once considered progressive become standard practice, e.g. checking their carbon footprint, recycling used paper at work, etc.

A distinguishing factor of Enlightened Red organisations is an abundance of space, time and energy to proactively consider alternative perspectives, rather than reactively respond to them, because the day-to-day takes care of itself. There is a wealth of physical, emotional, mental and spiritual health that permeates the whole organisation and business. Many business writers talk about this way of being within companies as thriving. There is a heartbeat, a rhythm and order, which we, as writers, articulate as flow because there is a clear vision, a set of values and full alignment at play. There's a sense of harmony: the CEO becomes the conductor conducting the orchestra.

Operating in Enlightened Red is a world apart from the acquisitive, materialistic space. Wealth and profit are still absolute essentials but the main differential is that organisations do not set out with that end in mind. The organisation knows its evolutionary purpose, its overriding why, which makes it easier to then align innate talent with a pioneering attitude matched with a desire to do social good.

Communism enabled a generation to envisage life without a monarchy and to shed the shackles of feudalism. The vision was to create a truly classless society; however, it was ahead of its time and the level of consciousness needed to breathe life into the ideal was missing. Driven by their ego mind, leaders were seduced by power and used control to hold onto it. In a business operating under Enlightened Red principles, the idealism of Communism takes effect without the negativity.

Morning Star, a food processing business, is an excellent example of Enlightened Red. It counters the traditional view of a need for a hierarchical structure. For more than two decades, it has operated without a boss; employees negotiate responsibilities directly with their peers. There are no titles and no promotions, and everyone can spend the company's money. Each individual is responsible for acquiring the tools needed to do his or her work and compensation decisions are peer-based. This might sound impossible and yet this is very evident in this large, capital-intensive corporation with dozens and dozens of processes, with just over 400 full-time employees and revenues of over 700 million in 2014.

An alternative way of redistributing power is through holacracy, which is also Enlightened Red in action. Holacracy is derived from the Greek word 'holon', meaning a whole that is part of a greater whole. Instead of a top-down hierarchy, think of a flatter structure that distributes power more evenly. The most well-known example of a company transitioning to this way of working is Zappos, a billion dollar online retailer with 1,500 employees. They experimented with holacracy as a new way to organise their business. Most of the existing workforce (86%) bought into the experiment, which led to the creation of around 400 circles.[6]

CEOs who sign up for holacracy agree to cede some level of power: the advantage is that they are able to view their company through an entirely different lens. They will recognise and want to move away from the limits of a conventional corporate structure. These companies are not leaderless – it is simply that individuals take personal responsibility for their work. Everyone is expected to lead and be an entrepreneur in whatever position they hold.

Whilst the underlying intentions of holacracy are designed to facilitate self-leadership and decision-making, its complexity makes it largely unworkable and impractical. This can be seen with the numbers of employees now leaving Zappos.

Other examples of Enlightened Red are the social entrepreneurs who focus on profit linked with a long-term business vision that is directed at sustainability and projects that meet unmet social need. This is a significant stretch from the old paternalistic feel of philanthropic Benthamite thinking. Although the intention with both Benthamites and social entrepreneurs is similar, the outcome is very different. Now it is all about helping others to help themselves and encouraging them to develop their own entrepreneurial spirit. The reason Benthamite thinking and initiatives like the Welfare State did not lead to major shifts was because they were imbued by a consciousness that those carrying out the initiatives knew what was best for those that they were helping.

It is highly unlikely that companies can just make the leap from Red to Enlightened Red without looking at some of their underlying issues. This can be done by working through some of the other colours and working with the transitionals.

Notes

1. Taylorism is a theory of management that analyses and synthesises workflows. Its main objective is improving economic efficiency, especially labour productivity. Also known as scientific management, it was particularly big in the early to mid 20th century.

2. *We have to go from what is essentially an industrial model of education, a manufacturing model, which is based on linearity and conformity and batching people. We have to move to a model that is based more on principles of agriculture. We have to recognise that human flourishing is not a mechanical process; it's an organic process. And you cannot predict the outcome of human development. All you can do, like a farmer, is create the conditions under which they will begin to flourish* ~ Sir Ken Robinson (2010) Ted Talk

3. Martin Seligman is a leading authority in the fields of Positive Psychology, resilience, learnt helplessness, depression, optimism and pessimism. He is also a recognised authority on interventions that prevent depression, and build strengths and wellbeing. He has published over 250 scholarly articles and 20 books.

4. In 1979 Michael Porter wrote an article entitled "How competitive forces shape strategy." Read this abstract for a summary of Porter's thinking - https://goo.gl/1BI6QR5. See the following article in the Independent for more details - https://goo.gl/gdcjHq

6. A circle is a group of Roles that all contribute to the same Purpose. Every Circle has "core roles" (e.g. Facilitator, Secretary, Lead Link, and Rep Link) as well as other Roles doing the work. A Circle is treated like a Role with the additional authority to break itself down into sub-Roles.

The Transitionals (CHAPTERS 6-8)

Figure 5.0 The Transitionals

Within *The KK Systems* ™, our colour framework for business, it is a necessary step to proceed through the seven fundamental core colours. And during that journey through colour, there are choices, or crossroads, that take you on deviations that, in the end, lead back to your soul path. These deviations are dives into the transitional colours. The role of the transitionals is to clear the blocks that are found in the fundamental colours and thereby clear the way to an enlightened space. For example, an archetypal Red leader who has amassed material wealth through their own drive and achievement can transition to an Enlightened Red space once they realise that money isn't a god and that more satisfaction can be gained by assisting others to wealth creation and by using their own capital constructively. Bill Gates has done this with his foundation. At the other end of the continuum, there are those that have taken a less traditional route through life and who have gained many rich experiences along the way in the desire to find themselves and connect with their more spiritual natures. These people come full circle to the realisation that to live in the real world, they need to ground their energy and that it is positive to be able to take care of their financial needs and generate a healthy income.

By the same regard, organisational cultures who have not yet learnt the basic discipline of rigorous Red systems to enable a healthy cash flow and build predictable revenue streams will struggle with the very idea of understanding their evolutionary purpose or creating flexible working practices.

What we suggest is that the transitional colours – Turquoise, Coral, Olive Green, Pale Gold, Amber and Teal – are seen as stepping stones to the success that enables a leader and a business to evolve. They offer the promise, or portals, to access the new ways of being from which individuals, leaders and organisations can go deeper into the patterns of conscious awareness and understanding about the evolutionary process.

Throughout the next three chapters, where we look at two transitional colours in each, we refer to the consciousness of each colour. This is deliberate because these transitional colours operate at a higher frequency than the seven foundational colours. For this reason we discuss the various attributes of each transitional colour rather than give you the positive and negative of each one, which would paint a picture that is far too simplistic and not give you the richness of each colour.

CHAPTER 6:

Turquoise and Coral

Turquoise

Figure 5.1 The Transitionals: Turquoise

For our description of the transitional colours, we are going to begin with Turquoise, which, as the first colour in this spectrum, is the awakening to higher states of awareness that lead to knowing. This is why we have offered an expansive description to aid depth of understanding and clarity.

One analogy is to see Turquoise as the ocean representing the hidden depths of human potential. Expanding on this, it is about waking to super consciousness which is that level of awareness that humans are able to experience when their mind is in a totally calm and uplifted state. This is what we classify as soul consciousness as opposed to ego consciousness, and we will take a deeper look at this later within this chapter. For clarity's sake this goes beyond the unconscious. This is the hidden mechanism at work behind intuition, spiritual and physical healing – it gives access to quantum leaps for innovation. We access the super consciousness through the collective consciousness which we connect to through the right brain.

Einstein captured this well: *The intellect has little to do on the road to discovery. There comes a leap in consciousness, call it intuition or what you will, the solution comes to you and you don't know how or why. The truly valuable thing is the intuition.* As we proceed through this chapter, we would like you to keep uppermost in your mind that Turquoise relates to the sixth sense, the invisible realm that moves us as leaders from *being* it to *knowing* it. Therefore, when we come to doing, it is much higher quality and so more effective, which is why Turquoise's mantra is "Less is definitely more."

At the core of this transitional colour is a clear *knowing* of the importance and power that emotions have in individual congruency of behaviour and organisational alignment of vision and values. This explains why we can achieve far more with less effort – we know exactly where to focus our attention point and can tune into the right place to make decisions.

Leaders who operate from a Turquoise perspective are few in number. This is because the current paradigm places more value on understanding experiences in life through the primary senses of what we see and hear because those appear to be more quantifiable and are assumed to be more reliable. Often leaders are so caught up with the mood of the organisation, their preconceived opinions, prejudices and beliefs, as well as what those around them think, that they dismiss their own hunches. And that is at their peril. Although intuition is now becoming more of a key element and a requirement in business thinking, it is still regarded with scepticism and too easily dismissed in preference for the purely rational factual view.

An example of a business leader in Turquoise is that of Dame Stephanie Shirley. She is one of the most inspirational women of our times: a former IT entrepreneur turned philanthropist who is now a champion of great causes.

An unaccompanied war refugee from Germany, she arrived in Britain when she was five years old in 1939, and found safety in a loving foster family. She always vowed to repay them by living a life that had been "worthy of saving". She went on to defy all convention. Having been rebuffed by the sexism in the workplace, she started one of the earliest software companies – what would later become Xansa Plc (now part of the Sopra Group) – from her kitchen table with only £6 of capital. In 25 years as its Chief Executive, she developed it into a leading business technology group, receiving her dameship for services to IT.

When bidding for contracts, she went by the name of "Steve" in order to overcome the prevailing sexism of the time. By employing almost exclusively women utilising a flexible home-based model and giving them the freedom to choose their own hours and manage their own workloads, she was ahead of her time. One might say that she intuited the future to bring into place such innovative practices. The company peaked in the mid-80s and Dame Shirley was worth almost 150 million pounds by that point, becoming one of the richest half-dozen women in England. As the business grew, she began to transfer ownership to the workforce, creating many more women millionaires in the process.

Her life has been one of extremes, both profoundly harrowing and extraordinarily successful. Her only son, Giles, at the age of two became unmanageable and within a week lost his ability to speak. He never talked again and was diagnosed severely autistic. As a pre-teen, Giles was placed in an institution. He never lived at home again, and died on 17 October 1998 from a fit that was a consequence of his autism. She herself has suffered from depression and a nervous breakdown and, on more than one occasion contemplated suicide. Just as in *The Little Prince*, our parable for Turquoise, Dame Stephanie had to make peace with early childhood pain, the later rejection from her surviving parents, and the continual struggle of living with a violent son with extreme autism. She had to conquer her inner demons to create an almost magical business environment and be at her best. Encapsulated within her autobiography entitled *Let It Go* is an extraordinary tale of creativity, resilience and generosity.

Turquoise correlates with the higher heart, which is located between the heart and the throat chakra in the Chakra system. We refer you to some of the research regarding heart intelligence that has come out of the Heartmath Institute in America, as this will help to explain the significance of this frequency.

Heart intelligence is the flow of intuitive awareness, understanding and inner guidance that we experience when the mind and emotions are brought into coherent alignment with the heart. The more coherent we are, the more we are able to pay attention to this deeper intuitive guidance. According to the Heartmath Institute, heart intelligence underlies cellular organisation and guides and evolves organisms towards increased order, awareness and coherence of their bodies' systems. When we are in a coherent state – from a physics perspective – virtually no energy is wasted because our systems are performing optimally and there is synchronisation between heart rhythms, our respiratory system, blood pressure rhythms, etc. Personal coherence builds increased composure, more energy, clarity of thinking, boosts immune system function and hormonal balance. Once individuals reach a level of optimal coherence within themselves, they go on to achieve greater social coherence with others.

We do this quite simply by getting more intentional in our ability to generate positive feeling states such as love, compassion, generosity, optimism and joy, along with other positive emotions, and we are in a much better position to do that when we have found that inner peace within ourselves which comes with practice. And this is a core element of Turquoise.

In business, it is not uncommon for leaders to hire and build teams that reflect their own leadership style and culture. Such leaders may have deep sector knowledge and specialisms, but in doing this there is a real danger of groupthink, fragmentation and silo mentality, all of which present as stagnation and same old, same old. This is hardly conducive to innovation and fresh ideas – a vital element to business success of this century. For years there has been an over-emphasis on productivity and efficiency and the measurement of what is being done, which comes at the expense of allowing space for creative impulses that lead to breakthrough success. Interestingly, now there is a real call and appetite for greater creativity and innovation, a real Orange phenomenon; but that can only truly flourish in environments where there is full empowerment and the space and reflection time to play, the starting point being Turquoise.

There is now greater awareness and understanding that creativity unfolds when positive mental states are encouraged. This starts with a focus on play and ideas in Orange and becomes stronger in

Turquoise because of the crucial emphasis on feelings. This trend has become more notable as business has found ways to respond to the 2008 financial crash. We also see this in the way that performance is increasingly measured now: the emphasis is no longer solely on quantitative elements, and more qualitative measures have started to be incorporated. The measurements of engagement and retention are becoming increasingly important in the West along with life and business purpose.

Dan Pink, in his book *Wired*, begins to get to the heart of some of these key business issues. He talks about how the future no longer belongs to people who can reason with logic, speed and precision. Many of us in business today grew up in the 1960s and 1970s. We were preoccupied by the need to excel at school, thereby securing our university place, gaining a credible degree followed by some kind of a professional qualification. Those with linguistic abilities frequently ended up in teaching, those who were talented at science and mathematics ended up in the medical profession or accountancy, and if you had great verbal skills, then a path in the legal profession was most fashionable. In later generations, people became more technology-savvy, prompting many students to choose hi-tech subjects in preference to these more traditional offerings. Technological developments influenced many to pursue business school where they acquired their MBAs with the assumption that it would give them a leg up ahead of the competition for the best companies and roles.

The knowledge workers advanced and got rewarded for their left-brained linear and analytical abilities and theoretical expertise, but then the world started to change and evolve again. Today, those capabilities are still necessary, but they are no longer sufficient. In a world enthralled by outsourcing and one that is drowning with data and choked with choices, the abilities that matter most are now closer in spirit to the specialties of the right brain – artistry, empathy, seeing the big picture, and pursuing the transcendent. And this is also a core aspect of Turquoise.

Dan Pink refers to this new era as the conceptual age, reflecting the shift from an economy built on the logical sequential abilities of the information age to one that is built on empathic and inventive abilities. So the scales have begun to tilt in favour of right-brain thinking; direct causes of this are the impact of a rising Asia market, greater abundance and automation. Again this indicates a shift towards Turquoise thinking.

Given the migration of core routine elements to Asia such as computer coding, financial analysis, legal research and other basic tasks like call centre management, the West needs to get better at doing the more specialist work. Specialisation infers moving to a higher-level client and service consultation to retain margin and yet it is far more than this. Dan Pink hints at the need for the West to hold a higher vision for the economic evolution of the world.

Katherine Benziger,[1] author, explains why individual coherence is so important. Her work in the area of leadership profiling is holistic, placing great emphasis on wellness and the need to help leaders avoid "falsification of their true type". This occurs way too often in traditional personality profiling.

She believes many will falsify their type, and behave in unnatural ways in order to fit into a culture, and that this frequently leads to negative consequences on health, happiness, and personal effectiveness. Benziger's ideas about falsification of type relate strongly to the need for people to seek proper congruence and alignment between their own true natural personal preferences, style, and strengths, and those of the organisations and services within which they work. Organisations and employers need to be alert to these issues, both in terms of re-aligning their own values and aims so that they become more helpful for the world at large, and in helping their people to identify, pursue, and fulfil their own unique potential and destiny. Benziger's ideas are at the heart of this very modern organisational philosophy.

Seminal work on how to become a values-led organisation has been produced by Richard Barrett,[2] who represents the archetypal academic Turquoise leader. Here, we, as authors, share his Universal Stages of Evolution because it represents a key element of the work we do.

Mastery of the initial three stages of human development comes from learning how to become independent within our human framework of existence. This is called personal mastery. We must start by learning how to master our basic needs, (both physical and emotional) and then, depending on how successful we have been, we gradually shift our focus to learning how to master our growth needs (mental and spiritual). Personal mastery is about gaining control over one's conscious and subconscious fears and developing the appropriate personal safety and financial security, a sense of emotional belonging, and a sense of self-worth that comes with the appropriate recognition and acknowledgement. As we learn how to manage, master, release or re-programme our beliefs that keep us stuck in a fearful mode of being, we are then able to evolve to the next level of existence. We are then well placed to listen to the growth needs of our soul as opposed to being the slave to the deficiency needs of our egos.

Learning how to bond our ego motivations with our soul motivations corresponds to the mastery of the fourth and fifth levels of human development. It is at these levels that we would become concerned with the search for our true identity, namely the seeker who is observing their own thoughts and feelings during reflection as they seek the deeper meaning behind life's journey. The true self lies behind the parental and cultural conditioning and wants autonomy. This is where we would start to discover, and then see, the emergence of the authentic self.

Once we obtain the fifth level of consciousness, we are well down the path to purposeful work because we know who we are now and we know our innate gifts, value and talents. Synchronicities become a common experience at this level of soul evolvement as we expand our energy and start to resonate with others who share the same values and desires. It is here that we start to trust our intuition and begin making intuitive-based decisions. Learning how to deepen our connection to our soul motivations and cooperate with other people, thereby leveraging our ability to fulfil our purpose and find personal fulfilment, corresponds to the sixth and seventh levels of human development. At this level, a leader would typically move from independence to interdependence as they have learnt to integrate what they know. Their words, deeds and actions are in total alignment with their soul. Barrett calls this external cohesion and it is focused upon our ability to make a difference in the world and finally give selfless service – the polar opposite of operating from our ego nature.

In order to master each stage of development, we have to be conscious of what our needs are, recognising threats in the changes that are happening around us as they may prevent us from meeting these needs, and also recognising opportunities in the changes happening around us that may serve to satisfy our needs. Intuition is the key to enabling people to move from self-actualisation (level five) to integration (level six) and selflessness (level seven).

Barrett's framework details perfectly how human nature evolves as we, as colour therapists, understand it from a colour perspective, and is probably the model most aligned to our thinking and understanding. It is interesting to note that he, more than any other established leadership authority within the field, has grasped the Turquoise patterns of interconnections to inform his earlier observations and current world view. In doing so he has been able to innovate by building on the earlier works of Abraham Maslow and create a detailed framework to measure the spectrum of human consciousness. What we began to appreciate more fully when we researched all this is that he has a predominance of the colour Turquoise within his soul path.[3]

The Attributes of Turquoise

<u>Attribute 1: Idealism</u>

Those who are drawn to Turquoise have a natural innate creativity that wants to be expressed: writers are a good example of this. Turquoise consciousness also prompts us to aim higher and to take a more holistic, humanitarian perspective. It appeals to the idealists in society who are always looking for better ways to transform the world. It shows up as curiosity with the need to understand the underlying context and complexity of any given situation.

<u>Attribute 2: Flow</u>

Intuitive insight and heightened states of creativity and flow come from Turquoise. The flow state is also known as "being in the zone" and it occurs when you are completely absorbed by what you are doing. In 1975, in his book *Flow: The Psychology of Optimal Experience*, Mihaly Csikszentmihalyi presented how flow works.

The optimal conditions occur when there is a perceived high level of challenge with a matching amount of skill.

If challenges are too low, one gets back to flow by increasing them. If challenges *are too great, one can return to the flow state by learning new skills ~ Mihaly Csikszentmihalyi.*

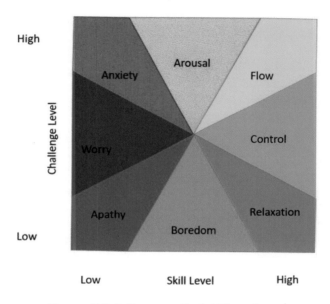

Figure 5.2 Csikszentmihalyi Flow State[4]

Evidence shows that the degree to which an individual is able to elicit flow states has more to do with the extent to which they have an internal locus of control, i.e. where they believe that they control events happening around them.

We are also more aware today that we are human beings rather than human doings and those optimal states of flow occur when we take regular rest and renewal time. In 2013, Tony Schwartz published an article called "Relax! You'll Be More Productive", which shows that taking regular renewal breaks every 90 minutes will increase your productivity and performance. Through The Energy Project, of which he is the founder and CEO, Schwarz indicates that there are four elements to increased performance: physical fitness, emotional happiness, mental focus, and spiritual purpose.

Attribute 3: Connectedness

Charismatic presence, connectedness and attraction are frequently found in Turquoise environments because flow starts with play and fun and being in the present moment – and those kinds of states are infectious.

If we can get to a place of intuitive-based insight without needing to feel that everything in the Universe needs to be materially measured and quantified for physical verification and evidence, we will not be weighed down by reams of data. That in itself gives us a lightness of being, enabling an empty mind to be inspired with fresh ideas.

Connectedness involves the need for the individual to have both feet firmly on the ground and an awareness of humanity's connection to the earth. As stated in the Enneagram, another profiling tool: when humans are born, they are perfect and innocent. They then learn coping mechanisms to deal with the reactions that they receive from those around them. Leaders need to become aware that these learnt responses and patterns of behaviour are conditioned behaviours. This awareness enables them to make more informed choices about how they want to feel and be as adults.

Our sense of connection expands with a conscious understanding that the higher self is connected to something bigger than we are (referred to in many ways as God, the Universe, Light or the sense of serenity that comes from observing a beautiful sunset).

This expanded awareness and connection allows a greater appreciation of Unity – union with others – rather than the opposite, which is separation and isolation. We only have to look around us today to see how often the sense of disconnection is prevalent and how the void is filled by overcompensating with the acquisition of material possessions.

Attribute 4: The Global Coherence Project (GCP) and The Global Coherence Initiative (GCI)

The GCP and the GCI explore interconnectivity/ interconnectedness, which is a Turquoise phenomenon. In many ways the HeartMath

Institute is a Turquoise organisation. In March 2012, an online paper was published[5] which explained the rationale behind the GCI, set up by the HeartMath Institute in 2008. It explains that the GCI is working in concert with other initiatives like the GCP to realise the increased power of collective intention and consciousness. The impact of 9/11 provides a concrete example of how this operates.

It is highly likely that you will be able to recall exactly what you were doing on the morning of September 11, 2001, the very moment when you first learnt about the attack on the World Trade Centre in New York. And if you were one of the millions who stared in horror at the television images of destruction and devastation from the toppling towers, you undoubtedly can recall the feelings you experienced. It was most likely a mixture of intense shock, dismay, disbelief, grief, anger and utter sadness at what you were witnessing.

You may be surprised, however, to learn that Princeton University researchers believe that so many people around the world were affected in the same way, at the same time, that the collective mental energy altered the operation of computers.

Those findings were produced by Princeton's GCP whose goal at the time was to determine whether, and if so to what extent, human consciousness – that is, our minds' awareness of the world in which we exist – can synchronise and act coherently. It turns out that the crisis, being the biggest event they had ever registered, ended up manifesting the potential to change the world.

The GCI has taken this further by testing a number of hypotheses to see whether human attention and emotion can directly affect the physical world and the mental and emotional states of others. This research gives a whole new meaning to the word interconnectivity.

At a business level, employee retention, engagement as well as innovative creative outputs are valuable indicators of social coherence amongst employees. It can often be very subtle. Recently the HRD of an organisation expressed surprise at the lack of complaints about the change in policy that had been announced without explanation by the CEO about month earlier. Employees showed their displeasure by boycotting the annual summer party (there were 60 attendees whereas the previous year 300 had attended).

Attribute 5: Intuition

Turquoise concerns intuitive-based thinking and intuitive-based decision-making, which thin slice data[6] and deliver the ability to know without fully appreciating why.

Being able to act intelligently and instinctively in the moment is possible only after a long and rigorous education and experience ~ Malcolm Gladwell.

In *Blink: The Power of Thinking without Thinking* (2005), Malcolm Gladwell explores the connection between cutting-edge psychological and neurological research and human intuition. He illustrates how thin slicing works by using the example of the J. Paul Getty Museum's purchase of a statue that turned out to be a forgery. Although the museum had some concerns initially, the sculpture passed a core sample test. Art experts looking at it once it was on display, started to express doubts. Through their years of experience, they felt intuitively that there was something not quite right about the statue. Further tests confirmed their doubts. How did they do it? As the quotation suggests, this ability only comes after years of study and practice.

Attribute 6: Compassion

The more we can tap into the underlying frozen emotions and heal those conditioned responses resulting from past emotional trauma, the more we find ourselves in a state of natural compassion for self and others. This overrides a tendency towards criticism and judgement of anything that lies outside our level of understanding and experience.

Attribute 7: Energy Characteristics

Turquoise has a certain masculine energy, whereas its complementary Coral very much represents the feminine.

Parable for Turquoise
The Little Prince

The following quotation by the fox helps us to understand the essence of *The Little Prince* by Antoine de Saint-Exupéry: *What is essential is invisible to the eye.* His story expresses our understanding as authors of consciousness – what we put our attention on grows, and the deeper we delve into our own inner world, the deeper we delve into the construct of thoughts, feelings and hopes. We then make peace with all of who we are, thus becoming more aware of our inner treasure. This is symbolized at the beginning of this parable with the drawings of the boa "from the inside" and "from the outside," indicating that within everything there is a mystery we must discover for ourselves. Beyond external appearances, there is the spirit that can only be discovered with the heart.

The spirit is what makes animals and minerals unique. It is the culmination of our choices, of our efforts, of friendship and of love. There are many roses that resemble the one that The Little Prince left behind on his planet, but that rose is unique because she is the one he has watered and protected, and because he has "tamed" her, to quote the fox, who added: *For what you have tamed, you become responsible forever.* The spirit establishes ties. To return to his rose, the Little Prince sacrifices his body, allowing the poisonous snake to bite him: *I shall look as if I were dead and it will not be true...,* he says, in his last message to us.

It is by the sum of all these efforts that The Little Prince has made his rose unique in all the world, and has come to love her.

The main character in our parable had to be a child because as they age, children lose the gift that allows them to live naturally in harmony with the spirit. As they become "grown-ups", their primary concerns are utilitarian. The material, vulgar side of existence traps them and they become victims of their own conceit, greed or intellectual laziness. "Grown-ups" judge what someone says according to the way he is dressed (as in the case of the Turkish astronomer), gauge the beauty of a house by its value and think they know a young friend by how much money his father earns. Because of this experience, when an aviator (who is perhaps "getting a little old") meets The Little Prince, he reconnects with his inner child. We need the spirit of the child in each of us to bring forth our Turquoise creative expression.

Coral

Figure 5.3 The Transitionals: Coral

The way to see Coral is as a fragile, decorative living organism on the seabed. We have used this analogy because Coral is a complementary to Turquoise and it is virtually impossible to access the hidden and sensitive depths of Coral without first experiencing Turquoise – which is the gateway to Coral.

Coral will give deeper dimensional access to issues that fall between Red and Yellow. Within Orange, for instance, there is a need for innovation and creative drive along with the importance of right relationships, whilst Yellow is overly focused on evidence-based decision-making with a clear structure. There is an overt tension – almost a polarity – between Orange's need to feel their way and Yellow's need for order. Coral provides a stepping stone.

For an illustrative example of emerging Coral consciousness, we will take a closer look at the evolution of the UK supermarket industry.

Through the 1960s and 1970s, it was more commonplace in the UK to purchase locally produced fruit and vegetables from a nearby store. The store itself acted as an informal meeting place for people to gather and catch up, as well as being a means of sustainable self-employment for the store owner. Suppliers in those days were predominantly local farm producers. Fast-forward to the present day and we have a monopoly of supply amongst a limited number of supermarkets. The ever-increasing demand to compete for market share has driven down the price, with both consumers and suppliers losing out in the process.

1. Fruit and vegetables typically travel a greater distance and so require more preservatives for longer shelf life.

2. A distribution system based around lorries and air freight has emerged, impacting adversely on noise and road pollution.

3. Perceived choice is a misnomer. That strawberries are available for 12 months of the year not only leads to confusion over seasonality, but also impacts on the quality of the product.

4. Variety within a category is seemingly promoted and yet the reality is quite different. When did you last see a yellow courgette in a supermarket or a cooking apple other than Bramleys?

5. The price savings that consumers supposedly enjoy need to be paid for somewhere and this is where suppliers often are caught within the bottleneck. They get trapped because the volume offered by supermarkets is generally greater than elsewhere, and in taking up what appears to be an appealing offer, they end up at the mercy of these giants.

6. Seemingly increased job opportunity is often packaged in zero-based contracts or unsociable part-time shift work that offers little reward and can be monotonous. It all comes at the expense of the independent retailer who cannot compete on price.

7. Today, we appear to have an increasing number of individuals suffering with food allergies and sensitivities along with rising obesity levels. Perhaps what we've been

enduring on the basis of greater choice at a cheaper price is having a detrimental impact on our digestion and relationship with food.

Tesco, up until recently dominated the market but in 2013 its profits dropped for the first time in 20 years.[7] For the three years following that dip it struggled to maintain market share and one view is that this is because consumers are increasingly aware of the company's dubious handling of its suppliers and favour Aldi and Lidl on price over Tesco.[8] This is significant because it portrays the journey they made as an organisation that focused on their price promise to the exclusion of other factors. In colour terminology, just like their brand colours, they had a passion for competition and the bottom-line cash-flow focus, one of the positive attributes of Red organisations. As noted, Green is complementary to Red and so for sustainable success, there needs to be an equal focus on what matters to all stakeholders. The Blue of their brand shows us authority within their field, but this has been overplayed and has led to a more authoritarian style of leadership with the supplier base that, under the surface, could be perceived as tantamount to bullying. One of the hidden aspects of Coral that can show up in less mature businesses is this covert and subtle practice.

Tesco focused on their strengths, namely efficient practices and processes with strong financial controls; however, when strengths are overplayed they become a weakness. An over-emphasis on cost, for example, is not sustainable in the long term. In the same regard, cheap food stuffs are not necessarily sustainable for our health and wellbeing.

When businesses operate from a positive Coral consciousness, there is an independence of spirit, an innate belief in self, clarity of mind and discernment with the recognition that, unlike Tesco, there is no need to be all things to all people. There is also an underlying wisdom and understanding about the balance of all the interdependent elements.

In many regards, Tesco became the ugly duckling, having once been the beautiful white swan. What the Tesco experience shows is that when Coral is overplayed, it leads to arrogance and the belief that there is no need to listen to others because you are the best. They now appear to have turned a corner: the question is whether they will be able to maintain this resurgence over the long term.

The Attributes of Coral

Attribute 1: Wisdom

Coral reveals to us hidden pathways of learning and understanding, yet its main job is a lesson in integration. One example of this is what can happen when an individual experiences an emotional setback. This can take them to a place of deeper self-reflection and if they happen to ask why, rather than get stuck in the grief, they can be rewarded with flashes of insight that enable them to recognise their deepest patterns. This process helps them to heal their inner child and thereby get back to that place of wholeness. In doing so, they interrupt the pattern, receive the wisdom and integrate the learning in Coral. In other words, it enables them to reframe their perception of any given situation and totally let go, which means they are far less likely to keep making the same mistakes. With a clear energy field and a better understanding of what they want to attract, they can begin to shortcut the process (in Turquoise) and begin to make wiser choices (in Coral). They are no longer weighed down with "should haves, ought tos" and regrets, and life feels lighter and brighter.

It is possible to have wisdom and knowledge, but often people have the knowledge without the wisdom. This is because knowledge is information gained through experience, whereas wisdom only comes when the information is integrated and there is congruency in the action. Wisdom is about understanding all the components at play, being able to decipher complexity and make the right decision based on a strong set of guiding values.

The real wisdom in Coral is learning the value of interdependence. When the ego is too dominant, there is a strong push towards independence, which can push others away. However, when there is a degree of neediness present in an individual, the pendulum, so to speak, has swung over to dependence, which also serves to put people off. The skill is being able to move beyond both of these to interdependence, which comes through self-acceptance and compassion for self and others; this only occurs when our inner belief in self has grown and the judgement has stopped. From a colour perspective, we see the element of Red, mixing in with Coral, which transforms into Pink which represents unconditional love.

Attribute 2: Self-acceptance

The difference between acceptance and tolerance is the difference between what we, as coaches, perceive to be real authentic power and the pursuit of power by force. In other words, acceptance leads from the soul level of consciousness, rather than from the ego level of consciousness. Acceptance is open heartedness and what you accept moves through your life without any resistance. Tolerance on the other hand, is judgement, which is a defensive stance. You think that you will not be able to change someone, and you decide to tolerate them rather than try to change them. When you decide to be quiet and polite in order to preserve the peace, for example, you are tolerating a colleague or your boss. You would prefer not to interact with them, but interactions are unavoidable.

Acceptance comes from the loving parts of your personality. Tolerance comes from the frightened parts of your personality. We judge others because we are separate from that part of ourselves that knows we are all connected. This is why there is tolerance instead of non-judgement. As you tolerate others, you tolerate yourself and your life at the same time, but when you can allow yourself to accept others, you accept yourself and others at the same time. Making the leap from tolerating your life and your work predicament to full acceptance of them and gratitude for all you have requires recognising when those frightened parts of your personality are tolerating in fear and when those loving parts of your personality are accepting in love, and consciously choosing love. You do not withhold your love.

Moving to a position of self-acceptance is a letting-go process which involves experiencing the pain and vulnerability of those frightened aspects of your personality that need to feel secure, needed and worthy; then, you can embrace the more positive loving emotions of true authentic connection back to self, and then others.

Attribute 3: Self First

Wisdom teaches us that true breakthrough success only comes when everyone in the organisation can recognise their own value and the importance of taking care of their own needs first. This may appear counter-intuitive to an organisation perceived as nurturing and one that puts its people first. Wisdom shows us that you don't have the capacity to coach and empower others fully without first truly feeling empowered yourself. Coral consciousness takes us into a fully mature business culture that does not need paternalistic Blue qualities or overly fixing Green qualities. This is because everyone knows their own worth and innate value, and they decide their own training needs and act on them. This is not a permission-based, nor is it a hierarchical, framework of authority – this is a place where talented people have integrated their work desires with their lifestyle choices and are fully accessing their intuition to provide regular states of creative flow. Imagine working in an environment where you are constantly appreciated for your unique input instead of hearing the constant reinforcement of how it needs to be. What would be possible from here? While facilitating, we have witnessed and believe that a greater sense of personal responsibility and willingness to own all of who you are builds greater connection and gives people the courage to take a stand for what matters. Ironically, the more people see our vulnerability and that we don't have all the answers, the greater the trust and the power of collaboration.

Attribute 4: Sensitivity and Body Wisdom

Sensitivity and body wisdom are two other characteristics of Coral. In an environment where each person's needs are honoured because there is full acceptance of the uniqueness of the individual, there is the space and allowance for the awareness of, and response to, the subtle shifts in the energetic field. This leads to a greater focus on the physical body, which is often the first place we feel changes in the vibration. Stress often shows up as rigidity in the body, as confusion and memory loss within the mind, and if ignored over time, these can lead to physical ailments that can be debilitating. Body wisdom is an invaluable early detector of individual climate control. This can also extend to an awareness of the collective mood. Coral integration work enables us to listen to our inner voice and have that present time focus; it enables us to access the place, which

161

we have come to understand through quantum physics, where we are able to access the collective consciousness because it exists outside of time and space. The more each individual can hold this state of being, the easier it gets to access universal wisdom, which gives ease to the whole process of living from the created self.

Attribute 5: Created Self

The underlying tenet in the created self is that all resources to solve any of life's challenges and business dilemmas sit within the individual. The seeker first has to learn through a process of dealing with hurdles and seemingly insurmountable obstacles that the answers and the energy of success are self-created through purposeful intention, directed focus and masterful discipline. The two main signposts along the way are self-acceptance and the recognition of one's own worth and value. The answers lie on the inside: we have to access our own inner hero to realise our fullest potential. To do that we have to make peace with our shadow self.

The same is true of business, of course: in a marketplace where competition on price has become an ever-increasing characteristic through the development of the Internet, we see the full impact of the erosion of value. For businesses to survive and evolve, they must continue to innovate, build an enviable reputation, and command respect in their prospective marketplaces. Competing on price alone will eventually seal the end of their life cycle.

Attribute 6: Courageous Conversations

It is only possible to have courageous conversations when we know that we are enough and so have a degree of emotional resilience that means we do not take things too personally. By the same token, the more we understand ourselves, the better able we are to connect with others to have those difficult conversations. We are able to listen for the feelings behind the words and facilitate the conversation so that all involved are able to find common ground on which to build a way forward. This is only possible when we maintain healthy levels of respect for one another.

Brené Brown, a well known author, researcher and public speaker, talks very eloquently about how courage is born out of vulnerability, which she discovered as a result of extensive research into shame and wholeheartedness. A key aspect to this level of maturity and self-understanding is to, as Brown states, *Acknowledge that we are "wired for struggle"*. We expanded on this in an earlier chapter where we explored the triune brain and the role emotions play in leadership. As a proponent for authenticity, she states that it is important to let ourselves be seen, deeply and vulnerably by others, and to love others wholeheartedly even though there's no guarantee of reciprocation. She also promotes the practice of gratitude to get us back to that wisdom of knowing we are enough.

The mantra for Coral, then, has got to be "You are innately creative, resourceful and whole". We end with a parable for Coral.

Parable for Coral
The Ugly Duckling

The classic 19th century fairy tale *The Ugly Duckling* tells the story of a duckling who, when hatched along with his brothers and sisters, is ridiculed and ostracised because they perceive him as ugly. He wanders alone through the autumn and winter suffering from fear, loneliness, and sadness. In the spring, he flies away from the marsh and meets up with a group of swans, and realises that he has become a beautiful swan. The story raises philosophical questions about identity and the nature of the self, the meaning of beauty and ugliness, perception, and the experience of solitude.

In summary, Coral consciousness is driven by the need for self-acceptance and self–worth and is fascinated by the quality of being wise.

The kind of leader who sits firmly within the Turquoise and Coral consciousness spectrum is a whole-brain thinker who can bring in the broader perspective. They have learnt the value of using their right brain first – for sensing, context understanding, pattern recognition and emotional expression – before delving into the linear detail and reasoning in the left brain.

Notes

1. Katherine Benziger (KB a Pub, 2000) *Thriving in Mind: The Art and Science of Using Your Whole Brain*

2. Richard Barrett, founder of the Barrett Values Centre, is an author, speaker and internationally recognised thought leader on leadership and the evolution of human values in business and society. He is responsible for developing the theory of the Universal Stages of Evolution, the concepts of personal and cultural entropy, and creating assessment instruments (based on Maslow's hierarchy of human needs and models of higher consciousness) to map the values of individuals, organisations, communities and nations to the Seven Levels of Consciousness Model.

3. In Colour Therapy, we work out a clients' soul path by looking at their date of birth and using numerology to work out their soul path in colour terms. Each bottle consists of two fractions of colour so to find three fractions of the same colour in a soul path is significant.

4. Adopted from: M Csikszentmihaly (Basic Books, 1998) *Finding Flow*

5. For more information, visit https://goo.gl/fOWfdc which provides a copy of the online publication in *Global Advances in Health and Medicine* written by R. McCraty and Doc Childre of the HeartMath Institute.

6. Thin-slicing is a term used in psychology and philosophy to describe the ability to find patterns in events.

7. Details are given in the following article from BBC news - http://www.bbc.co.uk/news/magazine-23988795

8. Reference is made on these points in the following article - https://www.theguardian.com/business/2015/jan/16/tesco-branding-consultants-fortunes

CHAPTER 7:

Olive Green and Pale Gold

Olive Green

Figure 5.4 The Transitionals: Olive Green

The natural precursors to Olive Green are Turquoise and Coral. There is no real separation from others. This is an understanding we grasp within the Turquoise and Coral framework. Turquoise enables us to understand that we are multidimensional beings connected to something bigger, and Coral supports us to integrate that knowing into a framework of acceptance and inclusion for all. It is from this place that we are able to step into Olive Green and accommodate everyone equally, as well as appreciate difference.

The simplest way to understand Olive Green is to think about the two colours that create it, namely Yellow and Green. Yellow represents the power centre of an organisation and Green represents its heartbeat. When these two traits are mixed together, the result is feminine leadership in the form of collaborative power.

What does the rise of the feminine look like in society?

A relatively small group of women have emerged who are shaping organisational development, and they have challenged stereotypical masculine perspectives to leadership. This started in the late 1990s with Margaret Wheatley's seminal work *Leadership and the New Science*, in which she presented on the interconnection of all things, including the critical importance of relationship intelligence as well as the opportunity to move towards a less controlled way of leading and being. This is at the heart of feminine leadership where abilities in connection and relationship building are well grounded.

Wheatley's thinking has spawned a wealth of similar initiatives from the Shambhala Leadership Conference in North America to the principles of *The Circle Way* by Christina Baldwin and Ann Linnea. The principle components of circle work are: the holder of the space who sets the intention before the circle is opened; the guardian who quietly observes the underlying dynamics within the group and will halt proceedings as required to facilitate deeper discussion and self-enquiry; and individuals who enter the circle with clear understanding of the purpose. Rich conversations of this nature delve into unknown territory that can trigger responses from the unconscious. Often individuals can make more sense of their whole selves and in doing so can embrace more of their shadow self and integrate that wisdom. This is critical work as we continue to evolve into the conceptual age where artistry, empathy and emotional intelligence take centre stage.

What is particularly fascinating about these movements is that for the most part, they started in broad community settings (for example, Parker J. Palmer, who created circles of trust as a concept, has worked with people in educational establishments for over 30 years), and have now moved into more traditional mainstream business environments. Another example of this is Susan Scott, who, in her book *Fierce Conversations*, provided the model used by PwC UK in the early years of the 21st century.

A way to see Olive Green is as a circle of creative feminine energy that provides new possibilities and beginnings. Rather like an olive tree, it offers us the promise of a new way of being as leaders in organisations.

The Attributes of Olive Green

Attribute 1: The Rise of Women in the Labour Force

The demand for women in the labour force was principally driven out of a shortage of supply, post WW II. These social changes created both greater opportunities for women and fundamental challenges for men. Fast-forward to present day and what can be observed is a growing trend of senior women who have left employment to set up and fashion their own concept of business. This means that there is an absence of role models within larger businesses around feminine values and styles of leadership. We'll shine the spotlight on the FTSE 100 and 250 Companies.

In March 2015, leading research by Cranfield School of Management revealed women's representation within the FTSE 100 Company boards to be 23.5% – very close to the 2015 target of 25%, with a shortfall of only 17 women appointments. If the appointment rate of one woman to every two men appointed is sustained, Cranfield University and the Davies Steering Group at the time of this writing expect the 25% target to be met imminently.

The FTSE 250 has also made great progress, more than doubling the percentage of women on their boards since 2011, from 7.8% to 18%, in 2015. The number of all-male boards in the FTSE 250 has also dropped from 151 in 2011 to 23 in 2015.

March 2015	FTSE 100	FTSE 250
Female-held directorships	263 (23.5%)	365 (18%)
Female executive directorships	24 (8.6%)	25 (4.6%)
Female non-executive directorships	239 (28.5%)	340 (23%)
Companies with female directors	100 (100%)	227 (90.8%)
Companies with at least 25% female directors	41 (41%)	65 (26%)

There are also eight females now holding Chairmanships of FTSE 250 Companies; the UK at the time of this survey ranked fifth in the world in terms of the percentage of women on its top corporate boards. Boards across Europe have become significantly more gender diverse over recent years. In Europe in 2014, the percentage of women on top boards varied from 5.2% in Portugal to 38.9% in Norway.

The Female FTSE Board Report 2015 Gender Diversity of Boards in 2014 - Trends across Europe[1]

Companies	% Board positions held by women	
United Kingdom	70	22.6%
France	58	28.5%
Germany	44	16.6%
Switzerland	34	13.9%
Netherlands	22	19.5%
Sweden	21	27.5%
Spain	20	15.5%
Italy	19	20.2%
Republic of Ireland	14	16.3%
Belgium	8	20.2%
Denmark	8	20.2%
Norway	7	38.9%
Luxembourg	7	8.9%
Finland	6	32.1%
Austria	6	10.7%
Greece	6	9.9%
Portugal	6	5.2%
Europe Overall	356	20.3%

Countries outside Europe have much lower percentages of women on their top boards than those in Europe, the key exceptions being Australia (22.6%) and the US (21.2%).

According to the report, the UK target of 25% has been strengthened by a number of supporting actions, which are:

1. The Voluntary Search Code has been implemented, whereby most leading search firms have agreed to a set of principles by which they will help to appoint more women directors.

2. Changes in the Corporate Governance Code have been made so that every listed company is required to publish its diversity policy and the numbers of women on its board.

3. UK Narrative Reporting is required by the Government, so that companies need to disclose the number of women at different levels.

4. Regular letters from the Government are issued reinforcing companies' success or reminding them of the need to change.

5. Regular research reports on progress are required.

It should also be noted that the statistics look healthier than might be expected, given the rise of turnover levels since the downturn of around 15% in 2008. This enabled the options of appointing far more women.

Peer pressure has also played its part, with one chairman in the report commenting that no one wants to look like a dinosaur:

I think nobody wanted to be left out, so once it became a direction of travel then people climbed on board because they didn't want to appear to be the odd ones out. The more people that did it, the more people saw that actually the boardroom dynamics improved, and they became advocates because of the improvement not because of the adoption.

On the issue of more women stepping forward into leadership roles, the report acknowledged the additional challenges women face. This begins to address the issue of whether or not leadership positions are attractive when the social stereotypes that act as obstacles to advancement are considered.

Aspiring to new ways of leading, interviewees in the report discussed leadership that encourages more affiliation and working together in order to achieve an outcome for the common good. Part of this new inclusive leadership comprised more knowledge sharing, openness, continued reporting and transparency pertaining to diversity at all levels of organisations. It also included pay gap metrics and creating cultures in which people work together constructively rather than compete narrowly against each other. This is most definitely an Olive Green-led conversation!

The research recognises that this issue is not just about board or even pipeline diversity, but is really part of a more substantive change process affecting the entirety of British business and its role in society. There is still some distance to cover as over 90% of non-executive directors are male. It will, of course, take some time to build the depth of experience which will enable that level of capability amongst the senior female working population. Most of the interviewees spoke of the need for systemic cultural change – at a societal as well as an organisational level.

Businesses are as much social vehicles as they are wealth creators. This is a direct reflection of the financial crisis which was born out of a short-termist capitalist, and narrowly competitive, model. Olive Green puts us in touch with a desire to share and contribute and become the agents of social change. There is a cleansing, almost spring-like, quality to this level of consciousness which provides a detox of the old to allow the emergence of a fresh alternative.

Attribute 2: Growth in the Number of Entrepreneurial Women

UK Female Entrepreneurship: key facts

1. Women account for under a third of those in self-employment, but over half the increase in self-employment since the recession started in 2008. Between 2008 and 2011, women accounted for an unprecedented 80% of the new self-employed (Labour Force Survey, Office of National Statistics 2013).

2. There are now almost 1.5 million self-employed women; this represents an increase of around 300,000 since before the economic downturn (Women in Enterprise: A Different Perspective, RBS Group 2013).
3. Women account for 17% of business owners, i.e. owners/ managers/ employers (Labour Force Survey 2008, in Women in Enterprise: A Different Perspective, RBS Group 2013).

Around 30% of all US businesses are majority female owned. The number of women-owned businesses continues to grow at twice the rate of all US firms, and they are increasing in economic clout. Women in the US are twice as likely to be entrepreneurially active as women in the UK. The entrepreneurial rates for men are roughly the same in the UK as in the US; we can conclude that any significant increase in business formation will only come from encouraging more women into business.

Many women have moved into self-employment/ starting a business; they have done this at the rate of five times greater than men because they are primarily responsible for child and parental care. A higher percentage of women-owned enterprises work part-time and directly from home.

While studies often suggest female entrepreneurs are held back by risk aversion and low confidence, in fact it is likely that this is not an individualised problem of self-confidence but more an informed assessment about how well prepared they are.

For the UK as a whole, women are more likely than men to be involved with a socially orientated start-up with 5.8% of women compared to 4.9% of men (Global Entrepreneurship Monitor Focus on Social Entrepreneurs, GEM 2004). Women are more likely than men to think that social, ethical and environmental considerations in business are important: 59% compared to 48% (A Survey of Social Enterprise across the UK, DTi, 2005).

The phenomenon of the increase in female business ownership and entrepreneurial activity has been made possible with the rise in access to, and use of, social media platforms as a mechanism for growing a business. This can only happen due to a Turquoise breakthrough with the growing development and appreciation of technological networks that lead to greater global connectivity. Women appear to feel more at home with social online connection and collaboration. Women are more biologically wired for social networking than men. Approximately 74% of all Internet users, at the time of writing this book, use social media sites and women are slightly ahead of the curve at 76% of usage compared with 72% for men.

Here are some examples:

On Facebook on average we see 55% more posts on women's walls than on men's; women have around 8% more friends than men. About 40 million more women visit Twitter than men, thus reinforcing that age-old stereotype that women love to chat and are the classic networkers in relationships.

The properties of Olive Green facilitate plenty of ideas generation and spark collaborative conversations as seen on all forms of social media. The danger of this is that as the social media sector continues to proliferate, people can spread themselves too thinly across far too many communication channels, thus diluting their impact and their message.

Attribute 3: Male Identity Crisis

As women's earnings have increased, a growing number of financially independent females have displaced males in their traditional role as the hunter-gatherers. This has led to confusion and a merging of roles within the family. At its most extreme, it has had a detrimental impact on status and can be divisive within society as men try to refashion their sense of identity.

More and more women are becoming the main breadwinners and in some cases rising into complete financial independence as millionaires in their own right. This has had a knock-on effect on men in that their traditional role models are being replaced and yet biologically they are wired to be the providers, defenders and protectors. Many are becoming house husbands or taking low-paid jobs; this has led to a male identity crisis.

One workplace response to meeting the desire for more women in senior roles in business has been to introduce women's networks and women-only sponsorship type initiatives. Conversely, this tends to have the opposite effect to what it set out to create. Women-only groups create clear separation of the differences between feminine and masculine leadership styles and there have been mixed results. This pattern of separation, however, has a useful function – it is one of the steps necessary for moving from dependency into independence of self. The networks serve to bring about collective cohesion. From independence, it is much easier to grasp the nature of interdependence, the ultimate goal.

As humans continue to evolve, we feel there needs to be greater recognition that the masculine and feminine live within each of us and that the way forward is to balance the two energies. If we are to give sufficient focus to being, and avoid burnout, we must take time to pause and integrate what we are learning. This, our failure to take the time we need to integrate, is the shadow side of Olive Green as it sits in Magenta, its complementary, which represents present time awareness as highlighted in Chapter 3.

Attribute 4: Rise of Metrosexuals/ Feminisation of Men

Feminine consciousness in society is not just the preserve of women. In fashion-conscious areas of society, we have seen the rise of metrosexual man. Typically, he is young, brand-aware with disposable income, image-conscious and into his body. Health, nutrition and skin care feature strongly for this individual. For identification purposes, think David Beckham and Alex Rodriguez.

A metrosexual male has been described as an urban heterosexual male from late teens to mid-30s who is self-conscious about his appearance and so is on trend and well-groomed. A metrosexual has a sophisticated aesthetic and often a well-developed feminine side.

We, as coaches, see this as a shift in consciousness, with males operating greater awareness of their feelings and femininity. Albeit a focus on the external, we do not believe this to be just superficial. Often consciousness shifts first appear as subtle signals that something needs to happen. This phenomenon is more apparent across a younger male audience.

Attribute 5: Characteristics of Feminine Leadership

Industry and work, as most of us know them today, were created by men; there are, consequently, protocols and mainstream established ways of working. We have all been conditioned to work in a way that aligns to male values. Businesses are focused on making money, working hard, being single-minded and individualistic. The focus is on being bigger, faster and stronger and it's all about winning, which is typically measured by how much profit is made. The typical job involves working hard at the expense of family, friends, and health and wellbeing. Getting promoted involves negotiating internal politics and ensuring that the boss looks good.

The crucial question to ask is: Does it actually work and is it sustainable?

The age of testosterone is receding as many more companies recognise and promote feminine attributes of leadership. Norway already have a quota to ensure that there is a female managerial presence in all of their companies and they have provided services for childcare to facilitate that, along with child-friendly policies that don't mean choosing the career over the family. This is one option to consider.

An Olive Green Leader and Company

One great example of the type of company in Olive Green is Audur Capital Financial Services, founded by Halla Tomasdottir. She has been instrumental in rebuilding Iceland's economy since its collapse in 2008. She believes that women's values are key to solving the financial crisis and to ensuring we never end up in such a position again. She believes that lack of diversity, overwhelming testosterone and sameness led to the disastrous events that set the world in turmoil.

Along with her business partner, Kristin Petursdottir, she applies these five feminine values to Financial Services:

1. Risk awareness – We will not invest in things we don't understand.

2. Profit with principles – We are not looking for just economic profit, but a positive social and environmental impact.

3. Emotional capital – When we invest, we do an emotional intelligence due diligence, looking at the people and whether the corporate culture is an asset or a liability.

4. Straight talking – We make the language of finance accessible, and not part of the alienating nature of banking culture.

5. Independence – We would like to see women become increasingly financially independent, because with that comes not just unbiased advice, but also the greatest freedom to be who you want to be.

Olive Green is commonly associated with due consideration for the feelings of others and the empathy to connect people. Relationship building and collaboration are natural qualities along with loyalty and commitment and a range of comfortable risk-taking. The current debate in business and within executive circles highlights reticence for the extreme risk-taking displayed in 2008 in the more male-oriented banking industry with its potential leaps in profit. The feminine way tends towards a more measured and balanced growth curve of performance.

In a world with a more even distribution of feminine values, perhaps the end goal would not just be about money: it would be about delivering a passion or belief first. Work could be more supportive, enabling both men and women to be successful without having to compromise on family and health.

The future is about a 50/50 female-value model – valuing collaboration, consensus-building and community ~ Cindy Gallop, Advertising Consultant and Entrepreneur.

N.B. We have chosen to cite majority trends above; there are exceptions, of course.

Attribute 6: Collaboration

For collaboration to be effective, the following pre-requisites are essential:

1. Alliances have come together because all parties appreciate that the whole is greater than the individual parts and recognise that each part has a unique offering to give.

2. There is full equality, yet no dependency, as each could stand alone if they so chose.

3. No side has pre-determined expectations around the outcome of the partnership.

4. A fully functioning healthy relationship embodies a maturity in the masculine and the feminine.

5. The feminine energy, seen as a circle of ever-expanding energy breathing life into new ideas, needs to be countered with the masculine energy of both form and function: the vessel holding the circle.

An over display of feminine energy yields great ideas but little execution and can often lead to indecision. And, too much masculine energy can overcontrol and lead to the doing and the how before full conception of an idea is realised. A direct consequence of an imbalance in either the masculine or the feminine within the partnership can activate feelings of envy, competition, jealousy, bitterness, dominance and control. The interplay in relationship is a great opportunity to develop awareness, but far too often what emerges is irretrievable breakdown through unresolved conflict. For the right conditions, the perfect balance of left and right, masculine and feminine, the giving and receiving of a perfect circle of energy are needed.

The mantra for Olive Green is "Many hands make light work", as it is based on the premise that everyone has something different to offer that leads to more, collectively. Yet far too often we see the shadow reflection at play, which is "Too many cooks spoil the broth".

An excellent example of Olive Green is Mary Robinson, who was the first female President of Ireland in the 1990s. Hers may not be a name that leaps off the page initially but that in itself is an example of the subtlety of Olive Green. When you delve further into her pedigree, you discover that prior to be being president, she was a civil and human rights lawyer whilst raising three children. Robinson lives by the belief that everyone does indeed matter and that what we do at this time – the decisions we take now – may well decide not just the quality of life for future generations, but whether those generations will even exist in the future on this planet at all. She has been called both the Ambassador, and a citizen, of the Republic of Conscience, an ideal and the title of a favourite poem of hers by Seamus Heaney.

We end this section with a poem by Oriah Mountain Dreamer entitled *The Invitation*. Oriah, first and foremost, is a storyteller whose life work has been the ongoing enquiry into the Sacred Mystery. She wrote the following poem one evening after returning from a party. She was frustrated by the superficiality of it all and the lack of deep, meaningful connection. She yearned for something more fulfilling.

The Invitation[2]

It doesn't interest me what you do for a living.
I want to know what you ache for
and if you dare to dream of meeting your heart's longing.

It doesn't interest me how old you are.
I want to know if you will risk looking like a fool
for love
for your dream
for the adventure of being alive.

It doesn't interest me what planets are squaring your moon...
I want to know if you have touched the centre of your own sorrow
if you have been opened by life's betrayals
or have become shrivelled and closed
from fear of further pain.

I want to know if you can sit with pain
mine or your own
without moving to hide it

or fade it
or fix it.

I want to know if you can be with joy
mine or your own
if you can dance with wildness
and let the ecstasy fill you to the tips of your fingers and toes
without cautioning us
to be careful
to be realistic
to remember the limitations of being human.

It doesn't interest me if the story you are telling me
is true.
I want to know if you can
disappoint another
to be true to yourself.
If you can bear the accusation of betrayal
and not betray your own soul.
If you can be faithless
and therefore trustworthy.

I want to know if you can see Beauty
even when it is not pretty
every day.
And if you can source your own life
from its presence.

I want to know if you can live with failure
yours and mine
and still stand at the edge of the lake
and shout to the silver of the full moon,
"Yes."

It doesn't interest me
to know where you live or how much money you have.
I want to know if you can get up
after the night of grief and despair
weary and bruised to the bone
and do what needs to be done
to feed the children.

It doesn't interest me who you know
or how you came to be here.
I want to know if you will stand
in the centre of the fire
with me
and not shrink back.

It doesn't interest me where or what or with whom
you have studied.
I want to know what sustains you
from the inside
when all else falls away.

I want to know if you can be alone
with yourself
and if you truly like the company you keep
in the empty moments.

More and more we are recognising that leadership is about being and bringing our whole selves to everything we do as well as showing a depth and care for our people. Margaret Mead encapsulates that very well in the following quotation:

Never doubt that a small group of committed people can change the world; indeed, it is the only thing that ever has.

Pale Gold

Figure 5.5 The Transitionals: Pale Gold

To fully appreciate and comprehend this transitional stepping stone, it helps to understand the colour components that make up Pale Gold, which are Pale Yellow and Pink. Pale Gold has an altogether greater refinement than Gold, which is Enlightened Yellow. It has an elegance – an almost royal connection – whilst at the same time a real simplicity to it. In Pale Gold there is a knowingness and understanding that we are creating our future: this is not present in the Gold that we met in Chapter 5. This can also be seen from the colour combinations used – Pale Yellow represents far more optimism and joy than Gold, and Pink represents love of one's work and greater capacity for unconditional, compassionate responses. Pale Gold pays attention to what is emerging and wanting to unfold.

This colour is the third in a series, which starts with Yellow, moves to Gold, which is then transmuted into Pale Gold. There is a common theme throughout this series, which is building ever-greater confidence in what is unfolding because the foundational work has been done on the inside. We also describe this as the individual's powerhouse, as it accesses spiritual energy, bringing it back through flashes of brilliance and anchoring it into everyday ideas and entrepreneurial business opportunities.

Pale Gold is the fully mature pioneer or entrepreneur: they have mastered the art of conscious intention and know that the future is created through them. They have let go of the need for certainty, other than the knowledge that their own intent is enough.

A Pale Gold person has real clarity about their purpose in the world and understands themselves and their deeper nature; they have integrated many facets of their shadow side. This person consciously chooses to show up authentically, and they radiate a powerful presence. Pale Gold sharpens vision and heightens an innate sense of self-belief, thus giving the power and the courage to be, then do, then have.

Within companies, a display of Pale Gold behaviour is stakeholder-focused as opposed to shareholder-driven: Pale Gold leaders consider their customers, employees, the community around them and the environment in every decision they make. They are the challenger brands with a compelling story often connected to some kind of conflict or tension with a protagonist and an adversary, as in David meets Goliath.

Often, their story is an anticipation of a future event whose outcome is uncertain. It epitomises the new kids on the block, the new order versus the establishment, the little folk who are rule-breakers challenging the super giants. A good example of a business leader who represents this is TOMS shoes founder Blake Mycoskie – the man behind the idea of One for One™, a business model that helps a person in need with every product purchased. Mycoskie appreciates that it's not just the right thing to do: it's also what will attract future talent to their organisations.

Pale Gold invites us all to be leaders now. The qualities of Pale Gold leaders can be seen in the following profiles:

1. The agent of change with a clear and transparent sense of purpose that invites others to join in.

2. The equalizer, who is taking from the few to give to the many by opening up great design or exclusive products and services for everyone, which are often characterized by

remarkable pricing or the deliberate sharing of knowledge that was previously known only to a few.

3. The maverick, who will use wit and humour to challenge complacency and mediocrity or political madness. They will be the game changers who typically create controversy and sparks wherever they go, in order to attract attention and convert others to a counterculture. Often they influence the way we live our lives as well as the way we think.

4. The champion of the people, who stands up for consumers because they have been exploited in some way by the establishment. These leaders will fight to overcome adversity on our behalf and invite us to join forces with them.

5. The authentic face, which appeals to us at a more personal level than the market-leader, partly because they reflect human-to-human connection as opposed to brand-to-consumer connection.

6. The enlightened soul, who calls time on low moral standards and behaviours, and challenges us all to do better.

7. The archetypal visionary, who focuses not on looking at what's wrong and building from there, but rather on seeing what the real benefit of their product or service is, beyond a functional level, transcending what is available in the market space.

The Attributes of Pale Gold

Attribute 1: Quantum Physics

Science in the form of quantum physics is now verifying what has been available in ancient wisdom for millennia. We now understand that at a basic level, we humans are nothing more than singular strands of energy pulsating in a universe of energy. Once we grasp this level of comprehension, we recognise that there is absolutely no such thing as coincidence, and that synchronicity is nothing more than focused intention and energetic alignment. In this place, we fully understand and have fully integrated the fact that we are the conscious creators of our reality from the inside out: this is Pale Gold in action. And when we know this, we apply a focused and seemingly effortless discipline and mastery to manifest the results we desire.

David Bohm, an early Pale Gold pioneer, is one of the most significant theoretical physicists of the 20th century, contributing innovative ideas to quantum theory, neuropsychology and the philosophy of the mind. His main concern was with understanding the nature of reality in general, and of consciousness in particular, as a coherent whole, which he stated is never static or complete but which is an unending process of movement and unfoldment.

Attribute 2: Spiritual Intelligence

The term "spiritual intelligence" was first used in 1997 by Danah Zohar,[3] and it is definitely an element of Pale Gold.

Spiritual intelligence (or SQ) can be described as follows. Imagine we are in the third lane of the motorway. Here, in this outside lane, we access a higher dimensional understanding and frequency, and through inspiration, we turn waves of energy potential on the spiritual plane into ideas on the mental plane of existence. Then, through our belief and faith in our abilities, we convert that energy into the manifestation of practical reality on the physical plane.
SQ is what people use to develop their capacity for vision, value, meaning and purpose in their lives. It has been little appreciated or utilised within the mainstream corporate world of business to date, whereas IQ, (intellectual intelligence), EQ (emotional intelligence) and PQ (physical intelligence) are well established and generally practised.

A high SQ is the best predictor for:

1. Vision
2. Positive energy
3. Flexibility
4. Fun
5. Happiness
6. Communication
7. Respect
8. Creativity
9. Serenity

10. Harmonious and loving relationships
11. Acting with a moral conscience.

As Zohar has highlighted it gives us our ability to use a multisensory approach to matters such as problem solving by listening to our intuition. SQ facilitates dialogue between the mind and the body. For example, if we know how to rely on our SQ, then we have more courage, are less fearful and more accustomed to relying on ourselves. We are more willing to face the difficult and the uncomfortable aspects of our lives. It enables us to live life more spontaneously and worry less about the uncertainty around our situation.

We use SQ to dream, to aspire and to lift up our spirits. It is, therefore, the ultimate transformative intelligence. IQ primarily solves logical problems and EQ allows us to judge the situation we find ourselves in and behave appropriately; but SQ allows us to ask if we want to actually be in that situation in the first place. Alchemy, therefore, is very much an attribute found in Pale Gold. Inner alchemy enables a person to transform setbacks into lessons, problems into opportunities, and pain into wisdom. SQ aids our ability to discriminate, giving us our moral sense and code of values, and allows us to temper rigid rules with compassion, acceptance and understanding.

Seen from yet another angle, our physical body is grounded within the third dimension and our energetic field, which surrounds our body, offers us access into the fourth dimension and beyond. This is the level of spiritual or soul intelligence; our right brain acts as a gateway to access the universal field of intelligence through our unconscious. When we can access the collective unconscious, we can bring back intuitive knowing to this reality. This is why SQ is the ultimate ingredient for Pale Gold pioneering territory!

Attribute 3: Shamanic Practice

Shamanism can be seen as the ultimate mind/ body/ spirit discipline. As we begin to expand our perceptions and awareness, we become more fully present in the world, and it's from the place of being present in the world that we create our reality. The energy of Pale Gold leaders is such that they are living examples of this ability to be fully present; they embody the "life force" so deeply that others perceive their charisma and want some of it.

Too much reliance on mental activities to discern what is real denies the wisdom of the heart, the gut and our cellular intelligence. This principle is central to the alchemy of transformation, as every thought creates a sensation and emotion. The shaman teaches us that we are not our thoughts and that when we neglect our bodies and suppress our feelings of fear and pain, we trap in our body the very things we seek to avoid.

Shamanism is one of the oldest healing practices on the planet; it is quite distinct from other religions or mystical traditions as it is not bound by any formalised set of beliefs or ideology. It is earth-based wisdom which draws upon the cycles and elements of nature and its wider relationship with the cosmos. Shamans have always known, therefore before quantum theory ever came into being, that everything in the universe is energy and that all is connected. They believe that the outer world of form and substance is created from within and, for perfect intention and manifestation to materialise, one has to transmute toxic thoughts, beliefs, emotions, assumptions and rigid mental constructs into loving self- awareness. Separation is an illusion – a construct of our perceived map of reality.

The word 'shaman' literally means "one who sees in the dark". Shamans enter trance-like states of altered consciousness to access non-ordinary reality or "dreamtime"; they apprehend information which is not accessible either in linear time or to the belief-based conscious mind. When they heal, their focus is on the energy field of an individual. They work with the root cause of an illness rather than just the physical symptoms.

Science has now caught up with ancient practice. Where previously it was thought that the nervous system was wired within the body with little switches that control everything this is not the complete picture. As a result of pioneering work to foster a leading alternative system of healthcare based upon the integration of biology and physics it is now understood to be a rather different reality. Research was led by Harry Massey's company- NES Healthcare Ltd. Massey's own interest grew out of his desire to overcome the chronic fatigue syndrome he had in his youth. The research pinpoints that genes do not need to control our destiny. We each have as yet untapped self-healing potentials and abilities that conventional science still treat as anomalies but that frontier scientists are taking very seriously. The new biology looks beyond DNA, genes and cells into the deeper aspects of what controls, regulates and directs physiology. One of the answers is turning out to be fields of energy and information.

Edgar Mitchell PhD (who set up the Institute of Noetic Sciences), Peter Fraser (the Chief Scientific Officer of NES Health) and Dietar Cimbal PhD came together to collaborate on *The Living Matrix* (2009), a film which shows us what the future of medicine and healthcare will be. The following is a direct quotation from the film:

The nervous system is transmitting a holographic message. The genes do not control our biology. Matter is compressed energy and information is merely patterns of energy. There is an information flow in our bodies, so the regulation of the whole organism and the coordination of all cells are accomplished with information fields.

Science has recognised that at least one third of all healings, including drugs, surgery and other allopathic interventions, have nothing to do with the process but have everything to do with the placebo effect – our belief that the intervention will heal us. Just as water in the Emoto research was influenced by energy, so is the information field and vice versa. It is both thought and emotion that create an information field. The human aura is both electromagnetic biofields and the informational patterns that organise them. Information fields react with consciousness. The brain is just a product of consciousness: not the other way round.

Therefore, whilst Science and Shamanism use different languages, they are in fact saying the same thing. Shamanism as a practice recognises both the power of intention and our abilities to use our imagination; it also teaches us, as do the other spiritual traditions, that words are vibrations that shape our lives. Magic is no more than the ability to transmute spiritual energy into physical manifestation. Indeed the word "abracadabra" comes directly from an old Aramaic phrase "abraq ad Habra" and translates to "I will create as I speak".

Shamanism is getting traction as more people look for their own answers to their life fulfilment and purpose and open up to exploring their inner space as a means to connecting with their higher selves. This is further indication that aspects of Pale Gold consciousness are gaining ground. We, as we work with our clients, are seeing an increased level of searching-type behaviour amongst leaders who are no longer satisfied with the concept of work and home as two separate entities.

Attribute 4: The Future of Work

As we move into what has been referred to as "the Golden Age of Consciousness," it is no coincidence that this is Pale Gold space – there is an increasing level of self-actualisation in the West in particular amongst the educated knowledge workers. The focus on self first, places the emphasis on who we want to be, which leads us to examine the quality of our existence and to create the conditions that are conducive to "soul work" which means living our life on purpose. This has led to an increase in self-employment, as this, at the moment, is the only way that gives people the level of freedom and flexibility they crave.

The idea of working from home with a mix of portfolio projects that produce an income is not new. The concept of portfolio careers was first introduced in *The Age of Unreason*, a book by Charles Handy, one of Britain's best-known management gurus, and a social commentator. In the 1980s and 1990s, Handy foresaw a world of flexible working and mutual trust that would free employees from organisations which he likened to "prisons for the human soul".
It's fascinating to see how, 20 years later, full-time employment is fast becoming a minority. One of the implications of this changing trend has been the degree of impact on lifestyle, with those sitting at the bottom end of the worker spectrum being forced into lower-paid, part-time and zero-based contracting, whilst the cultural creatives are actively choosing work-life integration to fulfil their creative potential. These categories are a world apart, and are at opposite ends of the colour spectrum. The cultural creatives are very much on the Pale Gold path and they want to thrive in every regard, whilst the others sit firmly within the Red survival category of existence.

Work-life integration is now replacing work-life balance as an evolving trend, and it meets this desire for self-actualisation, which is at the evolved end of the colour spectrum, where Pale Gold is situated. This trend has given rise to a growing army of free-spirited, entrepreneurial-minded folk who are working online, converting others to the idea of self-employment and portfolio working.

One of the most popular blogs in this genre is Pamela Slim's *Escape From Cubicle Nation*. Slim spent the first ten years of her business as a consultant to large companies such as Hewlett-Packard, Charles Schwab and Cisco Systems, where she worked with thousands of executives, managers and employees. Her first book, *Escape from Cubicle Nation: From Corporate Prisoner to Thriving Entrepreneur*, was released in spring 2009, and her new book, *Body of Work*, gives a fresh perspective on the skills required in the new world of work for people in all work modes, from corporate to non-profit to small business.

Attribute 5: Modern Day Alchemy

As previously mentioned, the Pale Gold spectrum is a concrete illustration of systems thinking in practice. Consciously and unconsciously, we are each members of many different systems and every act we take has an impact on one or more of those. However, the impact is often not that visible to the naked eye.

When acting from this intuitive Pale Gold space, life gets richer in every sense and the seemingly impossible happens almost effortlessly through grace, faith and through constant impeccability with one's word. One way to express this is through Arnold Mindell's[4] Three Levels of Reality model. At the top there is Consensus Reality, which is akin to everyday reality with its questions of what, how, when and where. The next level is called Dreaming, and it is where emotions reside – the deepest hopes and fears; the third level is Essence, which is akin to an urge. There are no words to express it but often there are bodily sensations that follow this gut response. If we capture it, we can shape it into a dream and bring it into our consensus reality. The model explains how we are co-creators of our reality.

In Pale Gold, trust is no longer a byword, as it is in society and in business circles today, because of the transitional colour steps that have already taken place.

Here is a short overview of these transitional steps:

If you recall, within Turquoise where we began our transitional journey, we explored the issue of idealism and the collective desire for better ways of being. One of the benefits of focusing on the bigger picture is that individually we get less caught up in the drama of our lives. We have this overriding sense of purpose and we believe that all is unfolding exactly as it needs to.

In Coral, we witnessed an emergence of the "self first" principle, which eradicates fears about showing up in any sense in an incomplete fashion. When this is fully integrated within a business or community there is full acceptance, because it is recognised that being your whole self is perfect and enough.

In Olive Green, we saw the power of empowered community activity, a deeper sense of the connectivity that binds us all, and where everyone is a leader and has a part to play in the dance.

Trust becomes obsolete within Pale Gold as everyone knows their purpose and can see how they fit into the wider, more intangible, collective conscience/ consciousness.

A Pale Gold Organisation

As an illustration of this in business, we propose a brief summary of the creation of Naked Wines, a company which was set up in the height of the recession in 2008 and was acquired by the largest wine specialist, Majestic Wines, in 2015 for £70 million.

So, what made Naked Wines so special?

Its founder and Chief Executive Rowan Gormley, an ex-accountant with a background in private equity, had already founded a number of high profile businesses, as well as Naked Wines. He was also behind the launch of Virgin Wines, the Virgin One account and Virgin Money.

The company is in effect a venture capital fund for wine producers and it lets its customers invest in small, independent, quality wine producers through the "angel" network, in return for exclusive access to wines at wholesale prices which can be as much as 50% less than the retail recommended price. There are no tie-ins or membership fees as a customer and the network now boasts over 150,000 monthly investors.

It is thus a win/ win for customers and producers, as angels, invest £25 per month into their Naked Wines piggy bank, which enables them to fund talented winemakers to make the wines of their dreams by hand.

Gormley calls it a "virtuous circle", where everyone gets more for less because the money goes to making wine rather than being spent on sales and marketing.

Naked Wines control the quality and service element by implementing a waiting list philosophy. This also adds to the "exclusive" element without implying snobbery and there is no membership tie-down as such, because Naked Wines believe the quality speaks for itself and that alone generates allegiance.

Part of their marketing strategy to individual customers includes a pack with personalised stories of the winemakers themselves so that customers can see the impact of where their money is going, as well as enjoy the product itself.

One particular heroic story is that of Katie Jones, a producer of full-bodied red wines, whose entire vintage of award-winning wine was destroyed when vandals broke into her winery. Two and half thousand angels invested in and procured every last drop of the remaining stock so that she could rebuild her livelihood.

Additionally, the business has collaborative friends such as Serenata Flowers: they pass on discount vouchers for fresh flower bouquets.

Operating profit in 2014 approached two million pounds on worldwide sales of 53 million, which had increased by as much as 40% on the prior year.

This business clearly took advantage of some significant shifts within the marketplace such as:

1. the rise of crowd-funding

2. a demand for quality wine at lower prices

3. capitalising on the growth and spread of the online social media space.

Its winning appeal came from doing exactly the opposite of what others were doing in the industry. Instead of screwing their suppliers, they decided to support them by giving them their first and subsequent orders before the wine was made – a strategy that had been employed by Marks and Spencer PLC in their early history of trading. With less need to focus their efforts on selling their products, the wine producers themselves could get on with the business of doing what they did best: producing fantastic wines.

Naked Wines is an example of a sustainable Pale Gold business model in operation. Gormley also ensured that the profits were shared with his staff by giving them an average pay out of more than £35,000 each. His business risk seems to have paid off very nicely for all involved.

The mantra, therefore, for Pale Gold has to be "Just be it, then do it!"

Parable for Pale Gold
The Midas Touch

The myth of King Midas is about the tragedy of avarice and narrates what happens when true happiness is not fully recognised. Midas was a man who wished that everything he touched would turn into gold. However, he had not thought that this wish might not actually be a blessing, but a curse. A basic spiritual tenet takes into consideration the purpose of our creations and assesses whether they are for the greater good or steeped in selfish endeavours. His greed invites us to think about and see the consequences that may lead us to become slaves of our own desires.

Atonement comes when we begin to realise that true fulfilment, connection and belonging only really come with sharing the wealth with others. Pale Gold consciousness understands this and has already integrated this principle from Gold to create the wisdom to build new states of being and wealth for all in the future.

Notes

1. Egon Zehnder 2014

2. This poem is by Oriah "Mountain Dreamer" House from her book, THE INVITATION © 1999. Published by HarperONE, San Francisco. All rights reserved. Presented with permission of the author. www.oriah.org

3. Danar Zohar (Berret-Koehler Publishers, 1997) *Rewiring the Corporate Brain*

4. Arnold Mindell is the founder of Process Work which enables individuals and groups to use awareness to track psychological and physical processes that highlight any inner conflict, and this can lead to resolution in the individual, the relationship and world work.

CHAPTER 8:

Amber

With Amber, we are building on where we came from. There is an impeccability in Amber that goes beyond what we experienced in Pale Gold, as Pale Gold is just one of the colours that make it up. There is a real depth to Amber that can only be fully appreciated when we consider the individual colours that define it.

Amber consists of Copper, which itself is a combination of both Red and Yellow, and Pale Gold. We get the grounding aspect of Red (a feminine colour representing Mother Earth) and the joy inherent within the Yellow (a masculine colour representing Source) to form a power pack. We then add Pale Gold, whose preoccupation is the creation of new states of being and broadening awareness, and finally Platinum, which is a fifth-dimensional colour and fire essence. This brings the contemplation and courage to be all we are can be.

There is little focus on Platinum in this book because it goes beyond the level of consciousness of 99% of leaders and organisations at this time. Suffice it to say that it represents the wise warrior locked inside each and every one of us. Platinum is the complementary colour to Pale Gold; in this regard, Platinum represents our ability to access that fifth-dimensional spiritual energy that facilitates the trust, grace and ease to live and work authentically. When we remain true to our highest values, we are in union with all things in the cosmos; otherwise, we put up a mirror of a reflection we care not to see, struggling with our commitments, living in denial – hiding our light and denying the shadow.

Below, we explore the richness of Amber by explaining the distinction between how Laloux describes it and how we see it.

Amber

Figure 6.0 The Transitionals: Amber

Amber takes us ever further on our onward spiritual journey of evolution and growth and is far removed from the amber model described within the integral theory by Ken Wilber and highlighted by Laloux in *Reinventing Organizations*. To serve as a reminder, integral theory documents the stages of evolution from egocentric consciousness, concerned with one's self; to ethnocentric consciousness, concerned with a tribe, nation or country; to world-centric consciousness, concerned with the good of all. Every ascending level of consciousness marks an expanding level of awareness and identity.

Both Wilber and Laloux, building on Clare Graves' earlier work, refer to the amber phase of evolution as the ethnocentric phase whereby society began to organise itself into institutions, bureaucracies and organised religions. They see amber consciousness as having the ability to acknowledge a deeper awareness of others' feelings. It is a move for greater social belonging. At that stage of existence, man could internalise group norms and the thinking dominated by it. Care and concern extended to the group of which an individual was a part, and the more scalable and organised the group, the more dominant it became. The Catholic Church is cited as the ultimate example of this type of leadership consciousness.

Amber civilisations therefore looked after their own and sought order, stability and predictability. This level of consciousness was based on the principles of immutable laws, of cause and effect and right and wrong. This level, say Wilber proponents, facilitated the systematic planning and organisational structures that gave rise to some of the greatest civilisations that built the Great Wall of China and the pyramids of Egypt.

Our model of Amber has a very different perspective. We see Amber as a consciousness unfolding right now and its main job is the focus on mastery from individual self-discipline. The amber civilisations of the past, advocated by integral theory, were run in an almost army-like fashion with strict adherence to a code of practice. It was this very firm discipline that gave rise to their success, stability and dominance. A crucial difference for us is that Amber is less concerned with dominance and power for control's sake and far more interested in the surrendering of one's ego to one's divine will. Amber focuses on aiding an an individual to master their behaviours so they absolutely fall in line with their words and every action. It is a subtle advancement on Pale Gold, whereby the frequency shifts up a gear, building even greater states of courage, collaboration, resilience, clarity, stability, tenacity, and acceleration of the manifesting process. It is certainly a stabilising process but does not resemble that of the old amber consciousness.

Acceleration

The greater your alignment with your soul essence when it is coupled with a focused practice of intention, the faster the acceleration process occurs, enabling ease of manifestation in present time awareness. In effect, this is really the embodiment of the 12-strand DNA,[1] or the fifth-dimensional individual operating in their homo sanctus state of being. The suggestion within the term 'homo sapiens' is that we are little more than biological machines. With homo sanctus, we are creating our reality as first introduced in Attribute 5 of Pale Gold (where we discussed why trust becomes obsolete because everyone knows their purpose and can see how they fit into the wider, more intangible, collective consciousness).

Here, there is some overlap with earlier theories, because Amber certainly recognises the importance of, and adherence to, the spiritual path. Far from separating others, as prior traditional forms of religions such as the Catholic Church, steeped in the teachings of sin and retribution have done, modern day Amber enables us to fully acknowledge and appreciate that we are the gods within. Once we embody all our light, there is nothing we are incapable of becoming. This definition lends itself far more to the ancient shamanic path of understanding than any organised form of religion.

This reawakening in the world at large is not a retrograde step into a past golden age, but represents a totally new integration of the three lower energy planes (the physical, astral and mental), into their higher counterparts, (the causal, buddhic and atmic). It is indeed the principle of heaven coming down to earth!

So that you can see how we increase our vibration and clear our energy fields, we need to look at concepts such as astral, mental, causal, buddhic and atmic which are subtle levels of reality beyond the standard five-sensory one. The rise of theosophy and anthroposophy towards the end of the 19th century offered a new era of spiritual science where many ideas from both East and West, both mystical and scientific, merged. Depending upon the system, there are between six and ten subtle dimensions, or planes of existence, in which human beings function.

The Physical Body

This forms the foundation of incarnation. At the physical level, the collective memory of humanity is stored in our DNA. Over time, the physical body more closely reflects the state of the astral body and its emotions.

The Astral Body

The astral body is the layer of the human aura that collects, stores and transmits all human emotion and desire from the ugliest to the loftiest. In the astral body, pain and pleasure are reflected as vibrational frequencies which divide the astral plane into "hell" and "heaven" realms. The astral body is most active when we are asleep, as it processes our daily urges through our dreams. The state of the astral body also has a massive effect on our health. After death, the astral body is directly confronted with the true nature of every single emotional impulse we had whilst we were alive in our physical body.

The Mental Body

This exists at a higher frequency than our emotions and it is constructed from our thinking life. This level is greatly influenced by the collective mental body of all of humanity. This plane of existence tends to pull our thinking down into those unfulfilled desires of the astral body. As our thinking turns to higher impulses, this body gradually disentangles itself from the astral body, taking on greater power. We can also use this body to repress the natural impulses of the astral body – this can lead to health problems at all levels.

The Causal Body

Often referred to as the soul, the causal body corresponds directly to the physical body but at a higher level. This body stores the collective goodwill of the human soul as a memory signature written in light. It forms the storage hub for all the high-frequency thoughts, words and deeds that we have initiated during our many journeys in incarnation. After death, the lower three bodies disintegrate and only that which is refined and pure is drawn up and retained in the causal body. The causal body, therefore, is responsive to higher visions and archetypal energies that lie beyond language, yet can still be conveyed by direct transmission to the lower three planes. It is a bridge between the higher and lower bodies.

The Buddhic Body

This is a higher tone of the astral body: it reveals the truth that humanity and all earth planes are one single organism. Once awareness is fully harnessed in the buddhic body, the causal body dissolves and reincarnation in the normal sense is no longer necessary. Through this body, individuals have access to the field of universal love and the higher frequencies often associated with enlightenment.

The Atmic Body

This is the higher note of the mental body, allowing access to higher consciousness outside the process of physical incarnation. The buddhic body retains its connection to humanity through its compassion, and the atmic body brings awareness into the cosmic field of Christ consciousness, directly merging awareness with Divine heart and mind.

The Monadic Body

The monad is the unconstrained primal essence of Divine consciousness itself. It enters the world of form through the causal body, which is the veil it takes on in order to enter the lower worlds; it corresponds to Divine will. At this level of advancement, each of the three lower bodies (physical, astral and mental) are absorbed into their high frequency equivalents (the causal, buddhic and atmic), thus revealing the true mystical nature of the trinity as three in one.

We are entering an era where more and more individuals will have direct access to an experience of higher consciousness and we're moving from an age dominated by "I" to one focused on "we". Amber consciousness is all about surrendering to that knowing and working from one's Divine will.

As Jesus Christ said, *The kingdom of heaven is within you.*

In bygone eras, it was precisely this insight that those in the know within the higher echelons of society – royalty, the church and many of the Intelligentsia – sought to keep from the masses. This gave rise to many secret societies such as the Rosicrucians and the Gnostics as well as the later Freemasons. Prominent figures such as Leonardo Da Vinci, Lord Byron and Sir Francis Bacon are cited as secret society members.

The Wisdom of the Heart

In earlier chapters, we touched upon the importance of the energy field in human development and evolved thinking. The clearer the energy field, the easier it becomes for individuals to intuit and follow their life purpose. We suggest that this is nothing more than being able to fully listen to the wisdom of the heart and work from the soul's intuitive intelligence, as opposed to relying on a purely mental construct of being. No amount of intellectual stimulation, accumulation of knowledge or willpower will take you to this place of insight and understanding, because it must be fully experienced and felt.

Willpower used in the wrong way becomes force and even though it may still succeed in its endeavours, effects on the physical body are catastrophic and often irreversible. This is because the body needs a perfect balance of homeostasis to remain in optimum health.[2] Any internal conflict that results from emotional and mental imbalance will tip the scales. So we may end up getting our own way and yet the separation that it induces can cause real emotional pain and friction.

In business terms, willpower is used all the time and, without adequate support from one's entourage, one may resort to force, or give in to compromise. This is rather common in the business world where leaders and employees work in roles with little or no sense of purpose and for fees that are far too low. The problem here is that when the spirit is not allowed the room to breathe or indeed lead, one ends up over compromising and settling, because on a deeper, unconscious level, one has sold one's soul and further reinforced the low self-esteem of the shadow self. On the other hand, when willpower is used as a force, there is an abuse of power, which gets played out in the work environment, as the bullies drive those with less willpower to breaking point. Employees leave or end up sick as a result of what has taken place and the ones in power frequently end up in isolation, lost in their ambitions and addicted to their work. Over time, this will drain energy from everyone and at its worst brings loneliness and isolation and finally desperation.

We'll take this idea further within the context of public services. Right now, the NHS is oversubscribed and has a massive deficit in spend. Reviewing this further, one begins to appreciate that some of the spending is the result of short term, reactive and rather chaotic planning. This is most pronounced when we consider the low numbers of available, highly trained doctors and nurses. The response has been to replace shortages via agency staffing, which has increased cost implications longer term and has a detrimental impact on the consistency of service. A similar trend can be seen in both the judicial service where there is a lack of available, experienced judges and the education sector which relies on supply teachers to meet demand. If we take this to a local level, we also observe this type of behaviour in the inefficient allocation of funds to maintain public services such as road and highway maintenance. Critical projects get placed on hold during the first ten months of the accounting year and then there is a surge of momentum in February and March when Council Officials are desperate to spend their full budgets to ensure the same level of funding the following year. This short-termism leads to poor decision-making and more of the same. Worse than this, it leads to a defeatist attitude as those in the roles think: *Why bother?* No wonder the spirit feels crushed and people lack the faith to feel they can affect the systems in which they operate.

Healing the Shadow

In order to start to embody all of who we are, ultimately light and frequency, we must first address our shadow self. This is the name given to those aspects in ourselves that we have disowned. Imagine a cave where you keep those parts of yourself in darkness that you would prefer not to acknowledge or own. This would include all your fears, shame, guilt, judgements, regrets and core beliefs, unconscious contracts/vows and truths about life, as well as your greatest power, your beauty and your sacred/divine self.

Once you make friends with your shadow, you open yourself up to your very own secret code, which reveals the programmes and patterns stored within your genes that dictate your thoughts, your feelings and actions, which give you your end results. When we heal our shadows from past emotional pain, which is often deep ancestral patterning, we release deeper authenticity, trapped life energies and inspiration.

Amber works deeply on the astral body and the soul's cellular memory. It supports us in opening to higher states of desire which are less focused on purely individualistic self-interest. Until we clear the astral fog of past emotional pain held within the ancestral lineage, it is impossible to rise above it all and act from a higher intention.

The Second Brain

There is a massive complex of nerve ganglia in the solar plexus area (stomach) of the body, which is often referred to as the second brain. It operates independently from the cranial brain. When emotions are at their extreme, the voltage generated here is far superior to any cognitive process of reason that we have come to hold in such high regard in business today.

Our emotions have more power over us than our minds and Amber helps us towards that emotional mastery and integration process because it allows us to make peace with our shadow. As we begin to integrate all those marginalised aspects of ourselves, we stop projecting our stuff onto others or judging that which we choose to reject in ourselves. We start to deepen our alignment with our highest selves and embody compassion for ourselves and thus, others.

Amber Leader

For a leadership example within the Amber spectrum of consciousness, we have chosen Barbara Max Hubbard. Known as the voice of conscious evolution, she is a unique and dynamic agent of social change. She is a social innovator, visionary and evolutionary thinker and believes that global change happens when we work selflessly and collectively for the greater good. She founded the Foundation for Conscious Evolution and in conjunction with the Shift Network, Hubbard co-produced the worldwide Birth 2012 – a multimedia event which was seen as a historic turning point in exposing the social, spiritual, scientific and technological potential for humanity. She has co-chaired a number of American-Soviet citizen summits, introducing a new concept called "Syncon" to foster synergistic conversion with opposing groups. Additionally, she co-founded the World Future Society and the Association for Global New Thought. Hubbard describes conscious evolution as an awakening of a memory that resides in the synthesis of human knowing, from the spiritual to social to scientific.

Parable for Amber
The Prodigal Son

The parable of the Prodigal Son is one of the parables of Jesus's teaching and appears in Luke 15: 11-32. In the story the father has two sons. The younger son asks his father for his inheritance before the father dies and the father agrees. He leaves home for a foreign country, but ends up destitute after wasting his subsistence with reckless living. As his money ran out, a famine occurred, and he went to work tending pigs, but even then he could not get enough to eat. He finally returns home with the intention of begging his father to be made one of his hired servants, expecting his relationship with his father to be irretrievably broken. The father welcomes him back and celebrates his return. The older son refuses to participate because he is feeling aggrieved about the thought of celebrating the return of his brother who has been inconsiderate, conceited and foolish. His preoccupation is with justice and equity and punishment of his brother for his misdemeanours. In many regards he is the archetype of someone who is outwardly dutiful and responsible, working hard but lacking the spiritual maturity and compassion to reconcile with his brother. He fails to recognise that anyone who claims to be in the light but still hates their brother is really totally lost in the darkness of their own shadow.

There is also the hint of jealousy that the youngest son who has done everything wrong is being celebrated. The father reminds the older son that one day he will inherit everything. But, they should still celebrate the return of the younger son because he was lost (effectively dead) and is now found. We get to see the opposite polarities of what the shadow side actually represents. It is not about wastefulness or being purposeless (the younger son) but nor is it about being morally self-righteous, judgemental and pompous (the older son).

The act of generosity and goodwill by the father signifies the spirit that can graciously give and forgive. This act of the father represents the unconditional love of the heavenly father who does not judge and for whom one's love is not dependent upon perfection.

It's a clever story of acknowledgement of one's errors and of the need to surrender one's will to spirit, working in harmony and balance with one's environment. We receive restoration and reconciliation as a result of that and the ability to co-create a fulfilling life. The younger son learned the hard way that the most valuable things in life are never those that can be bought or replaced. The dynamics involved are an alienation of the ego from the self, the conflict of the conscious and the unconscious parts and their reintegration through individuation; in other words the coming to terms with an important archetype other than the self, the shadow. The younger son leaves home because the ego must separate from the self (represented as the father) in order to achieve consciousness.

Such disconnection in the prodigal son leads to the alienation of the self from its greatest ally the spirit. In the squandering of wealth the son is illustrating that the ego has no real goals or commitments. The spirit archetype presents when one is in a difficult situation illustrating that spiritual growth and spiritual gold come from painful lessons where we learn to make peace with that destructive and fearful part of our self.

Epitomised within this story is the essence of Amber consciousness, in that our legacy becomes the focal point enabling us to rise above our fears and hold the space for others to find their own path. The mantra for Amber then has got to be "Embrace it all and hold nothing back!"

Notes

1. There are major changes and mutations occurring in our DNA. We are evolving and will be developing 12 helixes. This process seems to have started as long as 20 years ago; scientifically this is a mutation of our species into something for which the end result is not yet known. Scientific research has now proven that our DNA holds the genetic codes for our physical and emotional evolution through the frequency held in the languages we speak.

2. For a deeper understanding of consciousness and the part it plays in health and wellbeing, we recommend Richard Barrett's latest book (Fulfilling books, 2016) *A New Psychology of Human Wellbeing.* It develops his seven-stage leadership model to illustrate the impact of thinking and emotions on physical health.

CHAPTER 9:

Conclusion

This book packs in a wealth of information about colour and its impact on consciousness: its ability to heal both individual ancestral and corporate wounds. You have been exposed to the dualistic natures of the seven core fundamental colours and the initial five transitional colours and their deeper transformative natures. Colour has been our crucial stepping stone to this integration and wisdom and in this regard we trust that it has built a deeper awareness and more evolved consciousness within YOU, our reader.

One of the reasons we find colour so transformational in building sustainable results at an individual, team and organisational level is that it brings back that little bit of magic to the process of self-discovery. You start to see much more deeply how you are both the participator and the observer of your universe. With these keys you have access to the full realisation of your own and your organisation's potential. It is the glue that enables trust and understanding of one self and then of one another through the lens of one's own self-reflection work. As the energetic shifts begin to take place, we begin to see more visibly how the past and our unconscious emotions project us forward – recreating and impacting our futures. Then we change course through the process called intention, building the discipline required for personal mastery, self-reliance and interdependence. We start to see the invisible connections that are influencing the whole system which we occupy and we are able to unearth the ancestral ghosts of the organisation's past to resurrect or re-align the vision or lay to rest what no longer serves the present.

Our bodies and our conditioning have taught us that we appear to be separate. We appear to lead separate lives, to have different experiences, beliefs and opinions about what is true and right and how the world actually works. Yet this truth is only apparent at a surface level. Fear is what causes this sense of separation and so prevents connection and stops YOU seeing yourself as perfectly imperfect. Energy itself is never destroyed: it is merely transformed to something much more wholesome. Each of us inherits an ancestral lineage with wounds that need uncovering and then healing – be they victimhood, abuse and persecution, loss and/ or abandonment. As you transform, the energy of the entire lineage preceding you is transformed, for it is all happening now through you, as you. As your inner reality shifts, your outer reality harmonises, providing the perfect conditions for unity.

We appreciate there has been a lot to take in on the journey with us so far. Our focus in this concluding chapter is to distil and summarise some of the key themes.

In Chapter 1, we argue that the most recent catalyst for change was the Global Financial Crash in 2008. This led to an upsurge in interest in a new leadership and new business paradigm. That momentum continues, as the appetite for retention and engagement of talent has never been greater. Some of the main change agents are cross-referenced in the chapters targeting colours, because we see them as living examples of well-known leaders and organisations that model the characteristics and vibration of that particular colour. At the same time, we build on the main theses woven throughout the book, which are: that we are all here to acknowledge our feelings and that they have as much validity as analytical logical reasoning; and that we all want to experience how to thrive – not merely on a financial or material level.

We'll start with the first premise. On the face of it, it doesn't sound earth shattering until we examine it a bit deeper. Think about the workplaces you have experienced. To what extent has it been possible to express emotion? To what extent has it been possible to bring your whole self (that is all the parts that you love about yourself plus those "blind spots" (a technical term for the unintegrated shadow side) into your workplace? If you are really honest, then we expect the opportunities have been few in number. There is a simple reason for this. As we showed in Chapter 7, there is still non-parity between men and women at the senior levels in organisations. Most companies are run by men and whilst the gender gap is reducing at the top, the number of women on Boards across Europe in 2014 varied from 5.2% in Portugal to 38.9% in Norway. These figures show that there is still a way to go. Some men find expressing emotions, which are considered unacceptable in a public forum, incredibly difficult; consequently, they have created workplaces where the expression of emotion is actively discouraged – if not actually forbidden. Women have a part to play in this process of actually facilitating change. Typically when a boy child falls over, adults will say: *Boys don't cry! Man up!* This is one of the key reasons why so many men find it hard to be in touch with their emotions.

Non-parity is not a new phenomenon. Do you know why boys are dressed in blue and girls are given pink clothes and toys? During the Renaissance, the pigment which was the most expensive to make was pre-Raphaelite blue because it was made from lapis lazuli. (Synthetic dyes were not widely used until the 19th century.) Blue represented dignity and wealth, so those that could afford it dressed their sons in blue because inheritance passed down the male line traditionally. Pink, easier to make and cheaper, was allotted to girls. It's no wonder that still so many women have self-worth issues. This social conditioning has been ingrained through the different treatment of the genders over hundreds of years.

This can be seen so clearly with a read of Sheryl Sandberg's book *Lean In*, where the main argument is that it is tough to get to the top of organisations if you are female and that the only way women have made it in the past is by making massive sacrifices at home. Others have decided it is not possible to have a family and have a demanding career, and she outlines how many women have settled for lesser roles during the years before they have children because they feel they have to choose either to have a career or a family. For many, it is as if the option of having both is not available. Sandberg argues for greater diversity in the Boardroom and has started open dialogue around these issues to increase awareness earlier on.

Suppression of emotion also goes beyond the professional sphere. The current paradigm, as we pointed out right from the outset of the book, holds that nothing has validity unless there is scientific proof for it. In some ways, we, as authors, have bought into that paradigm in Chapter 2 where we explored the scientific origins of colour. The need for evidence is a masculine left-brained construct, which is based on the assumption that facts hold more weight than fiction or stories. And yet what is increasingly clear in leadership development circles is that the most compelling, charismatic leaders are storytellers and that it is stories which help to build the culture of an organisation. For that reason, we have incorporated parables and poems into this book because we believe it makes it richer. To be clear: we are not advocating a more creative approach over an evidence-based response; we are advocating the need for both.

In each human being, there is both male and female energy. However, the degree to which both energies are visible will depend largely on an individual's early childhood experiences and the extent to which they have integrated them. If, like us, you grew up in a house where analytical logical intelligence was prized above all, then you may also have, as we did, sought approval and praise through the academic route and by collecting more and more qualifications. That scenario highlights another element of our argument, which is that if you focus only on making changes to your external world, nothing will fundamentally change. You are likely to still experience a level of personal dissatisfaction. As we advocate in the book, the first step to change comes when you gather awareness of your patterns and how they are no longer serving you. The next is to find a mechanism that can help you affect change. Colour provides a way into wholeness and unconditional self-acceptance by raising individual consciousness. It offers leaders and boards a way of rebalancing their masculine and feminine energy both individually and collectively.

This book is calling leaders to increase their emotional range by focusing on integration as part of their learning journey. A great example of this comes from developing the ability to laugh at oneself. Laughter with – and not at – people is a valuable, helpful, and healing aspect of life. According to a University College of London study, laughter is contagious, even if you're not in on the joke. The brain responds to the sound of laughter and signals the muscles in the face to respond. Says Sophie Scott, a neuroscientist and researcher for the study,[1] *We've known for some time that when we are talking to someone, we often mirror their behaviour, copying the words they use and mimicking their gestures. Now we've shown that the same appears to apply to laughter, too – at least at the level of the brain.*

Laughter is a significant part of social connection, and some scientists believe our human ancestors may have laughed in groups before they could speak, making laughter a precursor to language. Part of the effect of "busyitis" is that some of that gentle humour is no longer present – today too many people take themselves far too seriously!

For this reason playfulness is a key component in the way we work especially now when leaders and individuals are more and more conscious of the adverse affect they are having on the world. This sense of urgency was considered in detail in Chapter One. It is hard to maintain a playful energy when we consider the impact we are having as a species on the planet's environment.

Another of the cornerstones in our philosophy, as we highlight in the book, is that whatever you focus on grows. As co-creators of our reality, we can therefore choose how this potential environmental catastrophe ends. The challenge is that a huge percentage of people struggle with uncertainty and try to avoid ambiguity. They are not acting, but reacting. However, from a systems perspective, order can only come from chaos. Currently we are living in a time of transition, which brings turbulence and options; another way to see two states is reflected in the Chinese characters for the word 'crisis': danger and opportunity.

Humanity is at choice to choose what to focus on, which is why, as we become more conscious, we become more aware of the words we are using and the mental strategies we employ to get to where we want to go. And we begin to understand that where we place the emphasis is where we will see growth. There is therefore more energy and expansion in moving towards what we desire than moving away from what we most fear. Conversely, when we are not impeccable with our word or we fail to find the courage to stand up to a bully, we perpetuate the situation and oftentimes make it far worse. What we, as humans, are being asked to do is to hold onto this polarity: know/ acknowledge that the world is in crisis – if as predicted, the population grows to nine billion by 2050, resources will be constrained – and at the same time have hope for the future, and actively participate in creating the world we want to live in.

Given the numerous books on how to find happiness and fulfilment, why aren't more people breaking new ground and living their lives on purpose? Our environment impacts us on a day-to-day basis and many continue to look for answers in the wrong places – outside of themselves – and this leads them to think that the answer lies there, on the outside. As leaders, then, we are taught to believe that it's all about action, and we engage too much of our time in doing, at the expense of being and reflection moments.

Leadership for the new paradigm necessitates a greater focus on leadership development itself. It calls for more awareness and intimate appreciation for who you are, how you frequently behave, what is deeply important to you and, rather critically, what you need in order to find true fulfilment in your life. When you are totally transparent about who you are and what you truly want, and what you find unacceptable, you will be seen as a leader with true integrity who can build trust in teams and the organisation as a whole.

We have stated earlier in this book and we reiterate here: it's not businesses that transform, it's the people. With this in mind, as a leader, it is not realistic to expect your culture to change unless you are first prepared to transform yourself. Cultural transformation must begin with authentic leaders who value humane business practices. When the top team leaders slow down to listen to the people in the organisation, and then act upon their needs, transformation itself becomes a much greater certainty.

Organisations are living, breathing entities – they are not machines to be systematically put together. Great cultures involve empowering and involving all the people through dialogue; these invite deep democracy, reflection and conversation to build collective awareness and unity. It's an emerging and continually evolving learning process of being and growing together. Healthy levels of interconnection and interdependence are required to build trust and to provide a sense of direction so that everyone feels that they can bring their whole selves to work.

Human evolution demands individual inner mastery and discipline to build heightened states of self-belief and possibility. This is only possible when people come to terms with their past. Humans are all naturally creative and whole, but some get lost in too much knowledge; some get lost in the journey home to themselves; and some who have had a glorious childhood can end up with massive egos and a belief that they can do and have it all. These are the main traps that prevent people from mastery and discipline and living the lives they were born to lead.

From an early age, we are conditioned to believe that the pursuit of knowledge and the gaining of experience will enrich our lives.

Whilst there is an element of truth in this, it is not the complete picture. If we engage in overthinking to the detriment of acknowledging our true feelings, then we are in danger of going round in ever-decreasing circles. This correlates back to increased stress, rigidity of thinking and mental health issues on the one hand, and an almost religious pursuit of happiness on the other. People have become obsessed in the drive for the end destination and the speed at which that will happen, rather than enjoying the journey as it unfolds.

As awareness increases, there is a realisation that it is imagination, rather than knowledge and experience, which holds the key to true freedom and power. Imagination opens the door to learning and curiosity, which are vital elements of an innovative culture. It invites everyone in an organisation to dream their world into being rather than getting lost in the consensus level of reality of the practical, everyday fact and reason that leaves employees feeling exhausted and burnt out. Visions are born out of imagination, and imagination requires stillness to listen to what the evolutionary purpose is and to set about its creation. We, as consultants, have noticed that many organisations get lost or are unclear about their way forward precisely because their employees are unable to articulate their visions.

We have defined state management as showing up congruently and coherently: where feelings and thoughts and words and actions are all aligned. This kind of charismatic presence is vital for leaders because it builds trust like nothing else and is the heart of engagement.

Human nature and the way we have evolved are such that we typically start out imagining the worst possible scenario because we are hardwired for negativity – the survival piece. This frequently plays out in business. In change management today, 70% of all initiatives fail despite lots of process, lots of action and lots of momentum. When we break down the reasons for this, it becomes clear that it is due to the fact that only around 25% of the participants actually welcome change – they are the early adopters. Around 25% come from a place of fear because they believe they are going to lose something rather than gain something, especially if they are not responsible for it. They believe the change will restrict their freedom, rather than enable them to be more. And the more entrenched that feeling is, the more they will subtly undermine the process. The remaining approximately 50% are reluctant to make a decision one way or the other until they have a clear idea of what is going to happen.

Underlying these types of behaviours is the question: "What's in it for me?" This comes from a belief construct in the West that the individual is all-powerful and can influence the outcome of any given situation. It is a hidden construct that is rarely challenged because it is an assumption that underpins every action. As we discussed earlier, planet-centric consciousness, or Teal, turns the question from "What's in it for me?" to "What's in it for me, you and the planet?" One of the principles that underpins this is that of engaged detachment.

This book barely touches on Teal. It was the focus of Laloux's recent book, but we see Teal very differently. This is because Teal can only be found on the fringes of society. It has yet to fully unfold. However we whet your appetite with a taste of what Teal is.

Figure 7.0 The Transitionals: Teal

Teal has a refined colour consciousness that is born out of its two component colours – Blue and Green. It heals the persecution patterns and aligns communication so that we can access and express the soul's intention. When we listen to our soul's calling, we can be fully engaged in our work, yet detached from the outcome at the same time. Non-attachment to outcome allows us to inhabit a reflective space where we can start to connect with what really matters to us and become fully engaged with it. From engagement, we can experience moments of flow and we receive the answers through listening to our inner wisdom and trusting the process, whatever it may look like from the outside.

Our next book will build on this introductory work and show readers how Teal is the entry point into new paradigm ways of doing business. It will reveal the full complexity of the KK Systems™ that we have only really touched upon in this book.

Right now, we are seeing the rise of the feminine as outlined in Olive Green in Chapter 7. At one level, this can be seen by the increasing emphasis of women taking more of a concerted stance in society. In business circles, the key word is collaboration. Across the country co-working spaces that are either free or low cost for small business owners are being set up. There is demand for these kinds of opportunities because there is increased awareness that when we work together, we can increase our impact and ultimately our level of profit. This is vital for micro-businesses. The fascination is not just at that SME level: it is also happening at the corporate level, where there is a realisation that large monolithic structures like BT do not have the agility of the Silicon Valley start-ups so the large corporations get round it by forming partnerships with these kinds of pre-IPO companies. But such partnerships bring other problems, often born out of the fact that both operators have very different drivers; these can be categorised as having either too much feminine or too much masculine energy. Imagine the feminine as being the ideas generator and the creative concept, and the masculine as bringing the structure and order required for execution. As stated in Chapter 7, when there's an imbalance, there are also feelings of dominance, control, bitterness, and more that, if left unchecked, can lead to irretrievable breakdown due to unresolved conflict. This shows that there is a fine art to partnership working and collaboration.

And here is where we stop distilling and summarising the themes in the book. (We hope there has been as much learning and growth for you, as there has been for us.) And we follow it with a distillation and summary of who we are.

As facilitators, our whole focus and attention is to enable greater connection and collaboration individually and collectively in order to build a more sustainable leadership and business paradigm founded on creativity and innovation. Our intention is clear-cut: to change the way business is done. As demonstrated in this book, we synthesise a wealth of materials from multiple sources that provides the inspiration to be and the momentum to change. Our purpose is to bring the extraordinary into the ordinary and to transform the ordinary into the extraordinary.

THE END

Notes

1. Details of the research into the laughter study can be found at:
https://goo.gl/t74RvP

Made in the USA
Charleston, SC
03 February 2017